Focusing with Children

The art of communicating with children at school and at home

Marta Stapert
and
Erik Verliefde

PCCS BOOKS
Ross-on-Wye

PCCS BOOKS
2 Cropper Row
Alton Road
ROSS-ON-WYE
HR9 5LA
UK
Tel +44 (0)1989 763900

www.pccs-books.co.uk

This edition published 2008

First edition published in 2003 by
Uitgeverij Acco, Brusselsestraat 153, 3000 Leuven, Belgium.

Focusing with Children
The art of communicating with children at school and at home

ISBN 978-1-906254-08-7

Cover design by Old Dog Graphics
Cover artwork provided by Marta Stapert
Printed by Cpod, Trowbridge, UK

Contents

Foreword

For the past few decades, the Focusing Institute has been teaching and promoting the Focusing method and technique to adults. With a network of over 800 Certified Focusing Professionals, it has a worldwide membership, holds conferences, publishes a newsletter, and has a large online library of research and articles. Marta Stapert, child psychotherapist, is the first to take this successful technique to children in the classroom and to the teachers. We are very happy with the result, and think you will be too.

Focusing is a natural process that was discovered through research at the University of Chicago by Dr. Eugene Gendlin, who became curious about why some clients benefit from psychotherapy and some do not. Collaborating with Carl Rogers, Gendlin analyzed many hours of tape-recorded therapy and found that the future success of the clients depended not on the therapist, but on something that happened (or didn't happen) inside the client. Gendlin found that from the very fist session, it was possible to predict which clients would be successful in therapy by noticing how well they were able to listen to their inner, often unclear, experience. Unsuccessful clients spent their time reasoning and describing their lives, and hardly ever paused to sense inside.

But what exactly were the "successful" clients doing?

Gendlin noticed that these clients struggled to grasp the totality of what they were experiencing. This totality seemed to have both a physical and an emotional quality to it. As the client "focused" on it, giving it attention and respect, it became clearer and a space opened up for new insights and unexpected possibilities. The inner experience changed and the change felt good. It was like a shift, a liberation. And with this shift, a change in behavior often arose.

Gendlin organized the skills he observed into a teachable practice which he named Focusing. To make it easier to learn, he broke the process into a number of steps, which he described in his book, *Focusing* (1978), which has sold over half a million copies and has been translated into seventeen languages.

In 1986, he founded The Focusing Institute, which helps people all over the world to learn this process and apply it to many areas of their personal and professional lives, including psychotherapy, philosophy, parenting, education, health care, management skills, writing, movement, and other creative arts.

The author, Marta Stapert, became acquainted with Focusing in 1985, when she was working in Holland as a child psychotherapist at a school for children with learning and behavioral difficulties. She writes, "Through Focusing, I learned to reach my own inside place in a more profound way. As a result, I could be even more open in my contact with children. I wished that I myself had been taught Focusing as a child, as a support for what went on inside me then.

"At the beginning, little was known about Focusing with children. But right from the start I noticed how natural a process it is for them. As I continued to use it professionally with school-age children, I saw that it deepened their connection to themselves, paving the way for growth and change. I also came to understand that Focusing is most effective when a parent or full-time teacher practices it with the child. With this in mind, I developed programs to teach parents and teachers how to bring Focusing to the home and classroom. The examples in this book are drawn from my twenty years of teaching Focusing with children around the world."

Marta has been certified by the Focusing Institute as a "Focusing Trainer and Coordinator". She gives training sessions to adults at Focusing with children in many countries around the world, including a biennial international conference on the subject. Focusing with children is now practiced in schools, hospitals, psychotherapy clinics, orphanages and in families all the way from Japan, Hungary and Romania, to Iceland and Suriname. Marta's articles, as well as articles by other authors on the subject, can be accessed through www.focusing.org/children.

The first edition of this book was published in Dutch in 2003 by Uitgeverij Acco, Brusselsestraat 153, 3000 Leuven, Belgium. In this translation, we have used the pronouns "he" and "she" fairly equally and have adapted some of the foreign names to make them more familiar to the English language reader. In addition, the chapters have been rearranged so that the main message is contained in the first seven chapters. The remaining chapters may be read at the interest and leisure of the reader. This latter half will enrich the reader's understanding of the program and applications described at the beginning of the book. The Appendix contains protocols and a bibliography.

The goal of this book is to help three groups of people: first, to help *teachers and childcare providers* all over the world improve the emotional climate in their classroom. After learning the Focusing attitude, teachers find that they can handle or deflect many problems by using only a few extra minutes of their time.

Having a clear social-emotional climate is the best climate for learning. Research shows that children concentrate and perform better academically when they do Focusing, especially when they do the first step of "Clearing a Space."

The second goal of this book is to give *school counselors* and *focusing trainers* a program to bring to the teachers and/or children. A six to ten-week program, meeting for an hour a week, is usually sufficient to teach Focusing to both teachers and children. With Focusing in place, other social programs, including programs for emotional health, have an increased and more lasting effect.

Thirdly, this book aims to help *school administrators* understand the significance of Focusing, so they can introduce and support this program. At first, school administrators may worry that the Focusing attitude will lessen discipline in the school, exaggerate problem behavior, or even force them to give up the rules of the school, which are grounded in order and safety. We hope that it will become clear that in Focusing you never give up things that are good. As you add Focusing to any other method or discipline, it gives more space and calmness to children and teachers.

Of course, *parents* will find this book useful in achieving a healthy and enjoyable emotional climate in the home. A special chapter (Chapter 12) is titled "Especially for Parents."

In a school or in the home*, the program must be voluntary.* In any given school, some teachers will want the program, others won't. The program can still work. Inherent to Focusing is that it can only happen on a voluntary basis.

Ultimately, this book is meant to benefit *children* everywhere. We want educators to know that children are quite capable of doing Focusing. We know that they are not blank slates that need to be written on. They have an inner life that, when listened to and encouraged, has the power to direct their lives in surprisingly productive ways.

If you are unfamiliar with Focusing, a prologue and final chapter describe the various steps of the technique in a way that you can try on your own. They also provide a review for those already acquainted with the process.

If you want more training in the process, the Focusing Institute provides Certified Focusing Trainers in many countries who are skilled at guiding newcomers through the experience either in person or on the phone. The Focusing Institute has found that most people "get it" in three to four sessions. You can go to the Focusing website (www.focusing.org) to find a lot of valuable information, or contact melinda@focusing.org or phone her at (+1) 845-362-5222 to find instructors near you. In addition, The Focusing Institute can help you find a local "Changes" group for people who practice Focusing or a Focusing partner with whom you can practice this technique at no charge.

The Focusing Institute
34 East Lane
Spring Valley, NY 10977, USA
Tel. (+1) 845-362-5222   Fax (+1) 845-678-2276
Email: info@focusing.org   Website: www.focusing.org

Prologue

What is Focusing?

Before you read this book, you need to be somewhat acquainted with Focusing, and that is the subject of this chapter. "Focusing is a body-oriented process of self-awareness and emotional healing [and growth]," says Ann Weiser Cornell in her book *The Power of Focusing* (1996). "Focusing is a step-by-step process of paying attention to a bodily sense of a situation, problem or creative project," says the Focusing Institute in one of their introductory brochures.

In the last chapter of this book, called *How Adults Focus*, you can read about each step of the Focusing process. These same steps are also described in Chapter Three, *Teaching Focusing to the Individual Child*, because Focusing is taught in a similar way for all ages. Prior to learning the steps, however, it is essential for the reader to understand the term "felt sense," which can be defined as "the subtle level of knowing that speaks to you through your body" (Cornell, 1996).

YOUR BODY'S WISDOM

What does it feel like inside of you? What do you notice inside yourself? If you want to get a picture of what is underneath a child's thinking and emotions, you need the ability to access emotions and experiences inside yourself. Then you can help children discover for themselves what is underneath. If you want to give attention to a child in a caring and open manner, you must learn to be open and caring about your own inner experience.

> *Imagine the following: You want to borrow an egg or a cup of sugar. You are standing in front of a neighbor's door. Get a sense of the situation in your body. Now imagine standing in front of a different neighbor's door. What does that feel like in your body? Are you standing differently? Feeling differently inside? All you are doing both times is asking to borrow something. But somewhere inside you is a complex knowing that changes the experience.*

Your body can sense a number of subtle distinctions that you might not put into words, yet your body knows them to be quite different. We call this the "felt sense" of a situation.

Frequently we are influenced by our felt senses, those subtle things that the brain does not name. Our body contains a more complex level of knowing than what is purely logical. Our felt sense can tell us a lot, but often we have forgotten how to trust it. In our society there is little encouragement for paying attention to our bodily-felt experiences. So we learn to ignore our body's signals and act solely on what our mind indicates is right or wrong.

Yet in sports we pay attention to our body's signals. We listen to the pounding of our heart after a 50-yard dash. We take it into account when considering whether to run another 50 yards. We pay attention when we are out of breath or our muscles are aching.

We also listen to our body when we eat. A hunger signal incites us to eat more. A full feeling tells us we've had enough. We listen to our body when we are sick, and we try to tell the doctor what is bothering us.

Then there are situations when our bodies tell us something of a different order, on a less conscious plane, such as when we are trying to remember someone's name. We say that the name is "right on the tip of our tongue." This can be an uncomfortable feeling. Once we remember it, the discomfort vanishes and we feel physical relief.

Numerous common expressions point to this relationship between our everyday experience and a feeling in our body. "It's breaking my heart." "I lost my head." "It turns my stomach." "He had a gut feeling," etc.

Often however the felt sense is vague. It's just an unclear feeling that there is something there. It turns out that by focusing our attention on this "something," it can become more distinct. We even find that this "something" carries meaning, even unexpected meaning.

We cannot control these inner sensations. Even when we'd rather not hear what our body has to say, it keeps sending us signals. If something is bothering us, it doesn't work to tell ourselves that there's no problem. Quite the contrary, that "something" remains present. By giving it a friendly sort of attention, this "something" can slowly become clearer and reveal some meaning. We do not have control over whether or not the feeling is present, but we can control whether or not we give it friendly attention.

Joseph is tormented by fear of getting cancer. Every morning he wakes up afraid he has a tumor. His friends and family try to ease his worries. The doctor assures him that, medically speaking, nothing is wrong. Joseph's wife can't understand his fear. Why should he be so anxious when there's no reason for it? She asks a therapist how they can get rid of Joseph's fear. She is dismayed when the therapist replies that the goal is not to take away Joseph's fear. While he is saying this, Joseph's relief is noticeable. The therapist says his aim is to make Joseph's fear concrete and to work with it. He uses Focusing to help Joseph stand still and experience his fear. Deeper than the fear of cancer, he discovers, is his inability to reduce his workload and make more time for his family. Joseph loves spending time with his wife and children, but as the primary breadwinner, his job is to earn the money to sustain the family. This makes him anxious. Just acknowledging this brings him physical relief.

Reflection:
Joseph's fear doesn't need to be suppressed. In fact, once he allows the fear to be present, he can look at what's underneath it.

By staying with the fear and listening to it, Joseph opens the door to change. Now he has a little more space inside and more energy for living his life.

What is a "felt sense"? It is:
- palpable in the body
- not purely physical
- more than what you can put into words
- meaningful
- sometimes vague, almost imperceptible

INNER MEANING

At the heart of Focusing is understanding that the "felt sense" of a situation carries meaning. Every situation, whether past or present, positive or negative, can give you a felt sense in your body. Usually this sense is found in your core — in the torso, that is, the stomach and chest — but it can also be felt in the throat, shoulders, or any part of the body.

Look inside you right now. If you notice a felt sense right away, ask yourself what situation in your life it might be connected to. Alternatively, you can choose a situation in your life and invite a felt sense to form around it.

Can you make the connection between your internal and external experiences? What is behind your behavior as a teacher? Behind your reaction to certain students or children? Can you listen to your own internal patterns? If you listen to yourself first, you'll be better able to listen to a child.

> *One afternoon, Marta presents an introductory Focusing workshop to teachers and staff at an elementary school. When she enters the building at 4 pm she notices a lot of commotion. The night before, the school was broken into and considerable damage was done. All day, the teachers have been busy with their students. This is the first chance they have to consider how the burglary has affected them personally.*

> *Marta invites the participants in her workshop to check inside for how Focusing could help. One teacher remarks that she's been feeling strange and grumpy all day and that the feeling interfered with her teaching. "It's as if I was in another world. Though the children needed me badly in all this chaos, I understood nothing of myself."*

> *Marta invites the teacher to check inside and notice whether her physical experience carries meaning, whether her grumpiness wants to tell a story. The teacher takes up the invitation and turns her attention inward. First she notices a feeling in her stomach. The teacher stays with it, giving it her caring attention: "... A mess ... No, chaos ... Chaos, that is the right word ... Voices are calling ..." She sees an image of a burning house and herself being carried from it. She feels her father carrying her. She sees horrible images. She hears voices and the roar of the fire. "... It is terrible ... I can still feel his strong arms ... I am safe ..." She sighs deeply: "... Now I can finally talk about it."*

Reflection:
> *This teacher's confusion as a child was never really heard. And even now that she's an adult, all day at school her old feelings had been rumbling in her stomach, distracting her. After Focusing she tells the group that no one in her family discussed that terrifying fire after it took place. She reflects, "Often I have a heavy feeling in my stomach without understanding why it's there. Now it feels so spacious inside, as if there's a hall there and I can dance in it."*

Focusing is a skill that stimulates more awareness of yourself. It is a gentle way of relating to your own inner knowing. Focusing teaches you to trust the wisdom you carry inside. It teaches you to listen to your inner experience while it is whispering, before it has to start shouting.

INNER DIALOGUE

In addition, Focusing enables you not only to listen to your experience, but to enter into a dialogue with it. By communicating with your inner knowing you allow for the possibility of change, the kind of change that is affirmed by an inner good feeling.

Focusing is not the same as venting your emotions. Our inner physically held experience contains a lot more than pure emotion. The felt sense may have an emotional quality, but there is more.

For instance, you may plan to have a calm conversation with your supervisor at work. But once you're in the room with him, you find yourself shutting down, forgetting everything you planned to say, or even yelling. This is not how you planned it. Afterwards, if you pay attention to what was taking place in your body, you may understand your reaction to the conversation, the meaning behind your behavior, and this understanding may give you a sense of what you can do differently next time.

Dealing with your inner knowing requires some daring. It is an adventure to be present with something that is as yet beyond words. Remember that Focusing is an innate skill but most adults have lost touch with it. It takes time to develop a good working relationship with your private self. It takes some searching and some practice to create a safe atmosphere inside, and to open yourself completely to what comes up. The good news is that the more you practice it, the more natural it will feel. It can be a pleasure to discover how simple and straightforward Focusing is.

> *Erik still remembers his first Focusing workshop. He was very tense because he very much wanted to do well and to learn a lot. Then the instructor said: "With Focusing, everything is possible. Nothing is a must. Your body will know where it wants to go." As Erik let these words sink in, he felt a sense of relief.*

You don't have to think. No analysis is expected. Of course, this is not to say that thinking has no place in Focusing. On the contrary, the felt sense is expressed through words, stories, sentences, or drawings. To create these symbols you use your cognition. However Focusing begins from a state of not knowing what will happen next. With this lack of knowing comes a certain vulnerability. It is therefore very important that you feel safe and learn to trust the inner process.

When we say that your inner knowing communicates by means of symbols, we mean that a certain word, image, or gesture will feel like the right way to express your felt sense. Finding the right symbol allows your process to reveal its meaning. Your inner knowing has a fuller, more intricate story to tell than you could ever think up.

> *Aurelie, a young woman of thirty, is attending a one-on-one Focusing session. She is searching for the words to describe her feelings toward her mother: "Open, really ... yet not the same openness as with everyone ... it is special ... my mother ... sometimes she disappoints me ..." As Aurelie says this, she digs her nails deeply into her hand. As she makes contact with a felt sense, she finds something that she can't quite capture in language; her mother hurts her. Through Focusing she is able to link this gesture with her hands to a felt sense about her mother; the gesture symbolized it.*

Fortunately, the body lets us know whether or not our symbols are correct. A correct symbol, or articulation, brings relief, while an incorrect one leaves us uneasy, with a sense that more could be expressed. A proper articulation of the felt sense brings an inner shift, a feeling of relief or peace and an end to any wrenching or pushing inside.

You can use Focusing whenever you need it. When you feel overwhelmed by emotions, Focusing ensures that you do not stay with their intensity. You can listen to the story of these emotions without drowning in them. Focusing can also clarify decision-making, taking you to a deeper level than you can reach by weighing options rationally or emotionally. If you are stuck in behavioral patterns, you can use Focusing to listen to the part of yourself that is responsible for those patterns. People who suffer from a lot of self-criticism can free themselves through Focusing. By Focusing you learn to accept yourself with all your limitations and possibilities.

In a wonderful variety of ways, Focusing supports you both in your inner life and in your contact with others.

The Importance of Focusing

INTRODUCTION

Simon has an ulcer, and he is only eleven years old. Simon's parents have consulted various doctors in search of a treatment. After starting a course of medication, the parents contact Marta, a child psychotherapist. During the first consultation, the situation seems clear. Other caregivers have already determined that the stress at school and Simon's perfectionism are the likely causes of the ulcer.

However, Marta's first consultation with Simon takes a totally different turn. As she encourages Simon to give attention to the tension in his stomach, nothing emerges about his perfectionism. Instead, Simon expresses his feeling that his parents — perfectionists themselves — never really listen to him.

There is only one person who can unravel the mystery of the ulcer, or any other emotionally based problem, and that is the person himself. The real truth lies, not with the physician, nor with generally accepted interpretations, but with the child's inner knowing. Focusing provides a way to tune into this inner knowing, through attending to — and trusting in — the inner felt sense of a situation.

Focusing is a special skill that helps a child explore the deep inner meaning of their experiences. On the adult's side, Focusing with children involves reflecting the child's words, while encouraging their contact with their bodily-felt sense. These skills can be learned by adults and children alike.

More than a set of techniques — although we will present several in this book — the power of Focusing lies in an *attitude* which we will describe little by little, using many examples. Once this "Focusing attitude" is learned — this attitude of being friendly to all that is there — Focusing can quickly be used to improve the emotional climate of the classroom. While a full Focusing session can take half an hour or more, the teacher or caregiver who has learned the Focusing attitude can use small Focusing interventions on a daily basis, to resolve many issues that would otherwise interfere with the child's growth and learning.

THE SELF BEGINS WITH THE BODY

A child's sense of self begins with his or her bodily-felt experiences. Babies learn that their hands — these seemingly free-floating objects — belong to them, that they can control their movement. They can cause their body to do things.

At first this self-awareness is only physical. The child experiences the self as "I am." Later babies discover a "self" in the realization that they can cause people to react or events to happen, and this opens up a whole new dimension. They can explore such questions as "How do others react to me if I drop a spoon?" "Who will come when I scream?" Later this develops into "How do I look?" "What do others think of me?" "What are my strong points, my weak points?" Self-knowledge of this sort is built up by interaction with other people and is influenced by the values of family and community. But the original bodily-felt sense of self is still there.

A child's sense of self begins very early, prior to language development (Stern, 1985, 1992). Up to approximately eighteen months, youngsters have a global perception. They do not distinguish between sensations, perceptions, actions, thinking, or other states of awareness. They experience everything as a whole. This sense of self is strongly linked to their bodily experience. Their body organizes and integrates everything without the intervention of thinking, and without much regard for the environment.

Stern feels that starting at about nine months, babies understand that they have their own world of experience and that others have one too. Sharing experiences then becomes possible and this changes the interaction between parent and child. Even before language is learned, babies begin to show their enjoyment of a book or activity, and parents can share this delight. However, while it is clear that the contact between child and adult plays a serious part in a child's sense of self, the internal bodily experience is still the starting point.

In their second year children begin to pick up language. This marks a big step forward in communication. But language also has its limitations. Although it allows children to share experiences, language also makes some aspects of their lives less accessible. Partly because they must learn to focus on a different set of cues, they learn to pay less attention to their bodily-felt sensations. And although language is useful and allows them to share what is going on inside them, it is often inadequate to express their experience fully. Also it is possible for adults to use language to mislabel or misinterpret a child's experience. So for several reasons a separation begins between a child's felt experience and the sharing of this experience.

Carla has just turned two. During lunch she munches happily.

Then she takes a sip of water and swallows too much. She coughs and makes a face. Carla's mother reacts with a joke: "It's nothing, eat some more and then your tummy will have forgotten all about the water." Carla continues to cough a little and then puts pieces of potato in her mouth. If Carla takes her mother's words to heart, then the next time she experiences something similar, she will tell herself: "It's nothing, if I eat something nice, everything will be OK."

Reflection:

Do you notice that a separation occurs between Carla's bodily experience and how her mother labels it?

What happens to a child's self-experience when it is not recognized or verbalized? According to Stern, even as children's linguistic sense of self develops, their physical pre-verbal self continues to exist. This sense of self, carried in their bodily experience, will always provide an important point of reference as they develop.

When adults observe children, they do not see what is going on inside, they only see the child's behavior. Yet they know there's a whole context to it, a history and background. Cognitive behavioral therapy teaches that behaviors are influenced by previous experiences, and not experiences only, but by how each person has processed those experiences. How people behave is determined by how each person interprets a situation. For instance, if a child screams, hides behind a chair and makes a face that says, "I'm scared," the emotion is caused, not necessarily by a scary thing, but by how the child perceives and interprets it.

However they are caused, emotions have a great influence on behavior. *Emotional intelligence* (Goleman, 1995) is, in part, the capacity for recognizing and responding to our own feelings, making use of them in communication and in the internal processing of our experience. This sort of intelligence is key to each person's social adeptness, as they reach out to connect with other people.

Most people can describe pretty well an event that has happened and the behavior that resulted. It is often harder for them to describe their thoughts and feelings.

Andreas' school is having problems with teasing and bullying and Andreas is called to meet with the school counselor. He is one of a number of young people invited to discuss the problems going on in the playground. In the course of Andreas' conversation with the counselor, it becomes clear that he knows a lot about what's happening in the playground. He clearly describes the coalitions that have formed among his friends. The counselor asks Andreas, "What happens inside you when you see that the group excludes Joran?"

Andreas shrugs. The counselor presses him, "Isn't there anything happening right now as you think about it?" Matter of factly Andreas replies, "Of course there's something in my stomach but what? I haven't got words for it."

Reflection:

> *Have you ever experienced something like this? Sometimes you know there are thoughts and emotions inside, but you can't find the words.*

You can help children make the connection between internal and external experiences. A child sees something upsetting and starts to cry. An external event has triggered some internal activity. That "something" is felt inside, but is not easily expressed. In order to express it, the child needs to move back and forth between thoughts, words, and that elusive "something" inside, in other words, to do what we call Focusing. This skill takes constant practice. If a child is encouraged to find the right expression, whether through words, drawings, or gestures, then the child learns how to share his experience with others, and in so doing, clarifies the experience for himself.

ADVANTAGES TO TEACHERS

In the beginning, teachers are often afraid that it will take a lot of time to give individual Focusing attention to a child. Then they discover how easy it is and how quickly both child and adult revert to a good energy state again, without loss of time. Says one teacher:

> *This morning, Michael hurt his hip during gymnastics. Previously I would have said: "Just go on; you won't feel it anymore." The rest of the day he would have disturbed everything in every way he could think of. This time I thought, "How can I do it using Focusing," and instead I said to him, "Your hip is hurting, isn't it? Is it bad?" He looked at me, surprised and a bit suspicious. I asked, "Where do you feel the pain?" Michael pointed at his hip and said, "It happened because Peter was pushing me." I said: "Is there something about it you can feel inside?" He replied, "Here in my belly ... but it's not that bad," and ran off to the other children. Nothing was wrong with him during the rest of the day. That saved me a lot of energy.*

One teacher discovered that raising her voice or delivering severe speeches to the child were no longer needed. She writes:

Since your workshop I've taken a new step. Often after playtime children came into the classroom very loud and boisterous. It was difficult to quiet them; only raising my voice seemed to work. Now I go and sit in my chair and pay no attention to them, but I focus inwardly. I feel my body in contact with the chair, I sense my feet on the ground and I concentrate on breathing. I ask the children to do the same and give some instructions. In a short time everybody can go to work quietly.

The complaint is that in many schools there are lots of extra programs. The teaching day is already so full with tasks and duties. Teachers have discovered that the Focusing attitude with its small focusing interventions actually free up time and energy for everyone.

A teacher had been warned about a new six-year-old boy, Benny, who had just come into her class. He was said to be angry and even dangerous. One morning she was nearly desperate, because he had disturbed the group all morning, talking out of turn and shouting. On the playground he had threatened other children with a knife. The teacher came to Marta for help. "What can I do, isn't this too complicated for Focusing? I try to be strict, reminding him of the rules, but nothing is working."

Marta said: "You must have had a terrible morning. Do you suppose we could feel with our empathic sense what is going on inside his small body?" The teacher said: "He must be very angry, maybe all black inside. It must be terrible to come into a group where all the children know each other. Maybe he's very lonely, but I told him to play with the other children and I spent a lot of time with him, didn't I?"

Marta asked: "How would it be if we reflected what he is feeling? You remember the Focusing sentence, 'There is something inside you that …' How about using that sentence repeatedly?"

The next day the teacher told Marta: "It's not easy going with him yet, but he's more quiet now and he's listening to me."

Besides freeing up time and energy, there are other advantages to teachers. When several colleagues are familiar with Focusing, they are able to listen to each other more deeply. They feel more connected and get more support from each other, speaking each other's "language."

Professionals who learn Focusing often experience positive changes in themselves. Their relationship with the children also improves, because they are no longer limited to telling them what to learn and how to behave, but are more in contact with the whole child.

Finally, teachers feel calmer inside. By clearing an internal space, they can occasionally create some distance from their work. This saves them much-needed energy during the working day. One teacher writes:

> Previously I could not get to sleep; my head was filled with worries and problems about children and parents. Now I am able to connect with my inner feeling of worry ... I put it aside and then I can fall asleep.

ADVANTAGES TO CHILDREN

Focusing provides enormous advantages to children themselves. As children learn to connect with their inner bodily awareness, they learn that this bodily feeling has meaning. They learn how to relate to and deal with their problems, instead of denying them or being overwhelmed by them. They learn that they may experience their sad, angry, or scary feelings, and that it is helpful to do so.

Children learn to clear a space inside by putting their bodily sense of a problem outside, by drawing or painting the problem, and especially by trusting their inner place that knows their truth or what is right for them. As they do so, they gain control of their feelings. One child learned to ask for help. The teacher relates:

> Mary (eight) stays on the sidelines against the wall while the other children are jumping rope. Spontaneously she tells me: "I'm feeling creepy itches in my tummy ... like a spider inside me ... who doesn't want me to jump ... but I do want to ... Could you help me to jump with the other girls?" Before this moment she had been too anxious to consider the possibility of help.

Because they feel safe and secure in a Focusing climate, they can concentrate better on what they are doing. Focusing makes it possible for them to keep their attention on schoolwork.

Finally, children who learn Focusing learn to listen to other children in an empathetic way. They accept each other more. They have a way to show their concern. Can we as educators ask for any better setting for their growth and development?

Of course it takes some initial effort to create such a climate. In the beginning of a Focusing program, the children may become rowdy or otherwise disturb each other. Maintaining the usual rules of the school is very important here. It is a change for teachers and children to go from "I know what good is for you and you will do what I say" towards "I trust you for who you are and together we will find your best way." But with persistence, the change will be good for everyone, and in fact, is urgently necessary.

Children's relationship with Focusing

Just like adults, children can listen to
their felt sense. They can describe where
in their body they experience things: fear,
disappointment, the feeling of always being
on the sideline, or of being bullied, the tension
before a sleepover, the excitement about a birthday party, or the
pressure they feel from adults. Through inner sensing, children develop
their unique personalities.

You may wonder, why teach children Focusing when there are
so many methods on hand already: social skills training, assertiveness
classes, and anti-bullying training? Why add Focusing as well? The
key lies in the words "as well." Focusing was developed as an
independent method, but it combines very effectively with other
interventions. When Focusing is added, these other methods obtain
more of the desired effect and depth. You don't have to throw away
any skills you already have. You can use Focusing in order to let
these skills come even more from the inside where true change
happens.

Here is an overview of some of the things that Focusing teaches
children:
- to make a contact with a felt sense or bodily awareness
- to trust that the inner sense knows something right for them
- to make contact with a bodily sense of specific problems
or situations
- to experience difficult, sad, angry feelings without either drowning in them or shutting them out

"Ouch! I have a
headache!"

• to know that it feels good to listen to
the felt sense, even when the sensations
are painful
• to learn how to express emotions in a
useful way
• to self-regulate feelings in each situation
• to clear a space inside by placing the felt
senseof a specific problem outside
• to concentrate better on daily tasks
• to remove emotional blocks to learning
• to know themselves better
• to know when to ask for help
• to listen to other children and to empathize with them, even in
times of conflict
• to accept other people and enjoy more harmonious relationships
with them

THE ADULT'S ROLE

Every child needs to be heard. From birth onwards, children are
oriented toward others, needing, even requiring, attention from other
people. Focusing is the best type of attention an adult can give. The
type of attention they get from adults will enable children eventually
to give themselves the same type of attention.

Initially, children are not capable of learning to focus without an
adult to model the process and show them the way. You can allow
them to lead as much as possible, or at least to set the tempo and
direction of the process, but at key moments you will need to offer a
suggestion or question that invites them to take the next step. You
will need to listen and mirror or reflect back what they say and do.
(See pp. 83–94 for additional description of *Listening and Mirroring*)
You will encourage each child to listen to their felt sense, until they
can do it independently. You can teach Focusing in a formal classroom,
a therapeutic setting, or limit yourself to the occasional immediate
problem.

Typically, Focusing comes naturally to children and at the end
of a short Focusing session, they feel very good, having found a new
way out of difficult feelings and situations. As their companion, you'll
be privileged to witness this small miracle again and again.

Gonda, a remedial high-school teacher, is asked to tutor Kris, a native Dutch speaker, in English. Kris is 15, dyslextic and convinced that he never does anything right.

In their first session Gonda explains how she plans to structure their lessons and what she expects from Kris. Kris is grumpy throughout, insisting he'll never be able to learn English. Gonda considers giving him a talk. She could say something like: "Don't you know what it would mean if you quit now? You'd have to repeat a whole grade and then you'd really be in trouble ... What do you think would happen to you then? What kind of work can you do at 15? Don't you want to finish school? You've been given one more chance. If I were you, I'd grab it with both hands."

But Gonda knows that this won't help. Instead of persuading Kris, she decides on a different approach for their second session. In spite of pressure from the other teachers to produce results as soon as possible, Gonda takes a risk and spends a full twenty minutes listening to Kris and mirroring what he says.

Kris: Listen, I haven't done the English homework. I don't have time for it.

Gonda: You didn't have time to do that lesson.

Kris: No way am I going to do that stupid lesson.

Gonda: No way are you going to do that.

Kris: Why do I have to do it anyway? They are all out to get me.

Gonda: It is as if everyone is against you.

Kris: I never do anything right here ... I am so sick of that.

Gonda: That sits there somewhere in your body like a sickness. (Moves her hand along her body.)

Kris: Yes, here in my stomach ... and that makes me so sick. (Punches himself in the stomach.)

Gonda: So sick ... there in your stomach.

Kris: It's the same everywhere ... Kris this and Kris that ... and that's why I don't want to do any of this. It's always the same hassle with English.

Gonda: Yes, every time you try with English something goes wrong ... you think that it will be the same here as it is everywhere else ... no one listens to you.

Kris: And that's why I am not doing it anymore.

Gonda: You're just not doing it anymore ... to make an effort to do something ... We're not going to do anything on it today. Next week I have time for you again. We're just going to move that homework lesson to next week.

Kris leaves hesitantly. He doesn't quite trust that there's no sermon and no punishment. He arrives for the third session grinning.

Kris: I did the lesson with my brother Miss. He doesn't mind helping me, because he sees me starting to understand it better.

Gonda: You did it together. And now you understand it better. And you are grinning as if it feels really good that you've done it.

The lesson was by no means without mistakes, but Gonda does not react to the errors at this time. She mirrors.

Gonda: You really did it now. How is that for you?

Kris: Rather cool really.

Gonda: Can you feel that "coolness" somewhere inside?

Kris: *Yes, it feels kind of nice in my stomach ... it's a bit shiny ... kind of content.*

Reflection:

• *Put yourself in Gonda's shoes. It seems as if the second whole session spent just listening was pointless. But in the third session Gonda sees that her listening did have an effect. Kris had found his own motivation.*

• *Would you have mirrored other parts of what Kris said? Re-read Kris' lines, and without looking at Gonda's lines, check inside yourself to see what your next sentence would have been.*

Just as in adult Focusing, the key steps remain the same:
• discovering a bodily-felt sense
• finding a handle and letting the symbol unfold
• resonating with the word or picture (the handle) until the felt sense shifts
• receiving any insight or change that comes

With children the whole process usually takes a short time. Children are often surprisingly clear about where they feel something in their bodies. Whatever wants to be heard frequently appears quickly. Children easily see the possibility of finding an inner story from their felt sense. But while adults use words to symbolize the felt sense in their bodies, children are more at home with non-verbal media: drawing, movement, and coloring.

WHAT CHILDREN LEARN THROUGH FOCUSING

Making contact with the felt sense
When children learn to make contact with their felt sense about something, they also learn that it feels good to listen to it

> *Micky is in her first year in school. She goes up to Miss Katrin. She looks pale.*
> *Micky*:   Miss, I'm not feeling very well.
> *Teacher*: Where do you feel that?
> *Micky*:   Here … *(She points to her belly)*
> *Teacher*: How does it feel there? Does it resemble a color?
> *Micky*: *(putting her hand on her belly)* It is dark.
> *Teacher*: How is that dark there? For example, is it like a mole's little hole or like a big dark cloud?
> *Micky*:   Hmmm … like a mole's little hole.
> *She skips off and is cheerful all morning.*

Reflection:
> • *Do you notice the difference between paying attention to the child and helping the child pay attention to what is bothering her?*
> • *Do you notice how fast Micky can move on, once the stomachache has been heard?*
> • *You can use this type of micro-process many times a day.*

Accepting difficult feelings
It appears that our society teaches children that they are not allowed to have certain feelings. But when children feel sad, frightened, or angry, it is for a reason.

How do you react when a child falls down on the pavement? Do you respond with a quick: "Well, it's only a few scratches," or "Don't cry; be a big girl"? Or do you deal with their feelings in a "soft" way, offering kisses and sweets for wounds and disappointments? Still others might advise the distressed child, "Go get a drink of water, then you won't think about it anymore." Adults often don't know what to do about children's emotions; they feel powerless.

But Focusing allows children to listen to these difficult feelings. It asks children to draw on their own resources and come to a solution themselves. This process can be supported by your safe presence as a Focusing companion.

Expressing emotions
Sometimes children appear to be entangled in a mishmash of emotions.

They may not know what they feel. Is it anger or sadness? They can't tell you.

boos zijn is oke

"It's OK to be angry"

What happens if an adult labels every emotional outburst of a child as "angry"? It would not be possible for the child to put another word on her feelings. Because you, the adult, keep translating it as angry, saying "Stop being so angry all the time," the child also labels these feelings as anger, which is usually something unacceptable to adults. But there may also be sadness in this outburst, or frustration or fear.

It helps the child if he can learn to take a step *below* the emotionality: what is the bodily-felt sense of the outburst and what does it have to say?

> *Sophie is overjoyed with her new bicycle for her sixth birthday. She wants to cycle to the park immediately. Her mother cycles behind her. Sophie enjoys it more and more; she becomes braver and starts to go faster. Mother, behind her, calls out: "Watch out for the bend!" It is already too late. Sophie can't slow down. She slips and falls and grazes her knee. Two girls are standing there watching without saying a word.*
>
> *At home Sophie bursts into tears. Mother does everything to comfort her, to talk to her, but Sophie does not stop crying.*
> *Mother:* Come here, I will put a kiss on your knee ... then we'll drink some lemonade. Maybe the bicycle is a little too big for you after all ... Shall I dry your tears? You were going too fast. Did you hear me call out to you? You shouldn't cycle so fast anymore ... I will get a band-aid .,. We will try again tomorrow, you can take it a bit slower.

> *The difficult thing is that Sophie continues to sob. Then the mother remembers what she learned in the course on Focusing with children. She changes her approach and helps Sophie discover from within what the essence of the problem really is.*
> *Mother:* Shall we listen inside together to hear what happened?
> *Sophie:* Yesss ...
> *Mother:* You took a really bad fall with your new bicycle, didn't

you? You were doing so well. You dared to go fast ... and now you have a scraped knee. And it hurts.

Sophie: *(continues to cry and sob)* ... yes ... yes ... yes ...

Mother: You also have to sob really badly ... Can you feel inside where that bad thing is?

Sophie: *(Points to her stomach)*

Mother: Can you sit with it in a friendly way and ask what it feels like there?

Sophie: It is in my stomach here ... really bad ... *(She becomes more quiet and attentive)*

Mother: It is in your stomach ... how is it there in your stomach?

Sophie: It's all going around ... *(She moves her hands around)*

Mother: It just keeps going around inside.

Sophie: Just like grabbing hands.

Mother: Just like grabbing hands ... If you keep feeling that, do those grabbing hands have a story to tell you?

Sophie: *(Sobbing loudly now)* Yes, those big girls should not have stood there looking like that ... I'm sure they think I'm a stupid little kid.

Mother: You hated that they were standing there looking ... they are bigger ... And then you are afraid that they think you are small and stupid ... Does that feeling have a color inside? Maybe you can close your eyes for a minute and wait for what comes.

Sophie: Yes ... red is coming ... and also something black ...

Mother: Would you draw and color it? Your hand will put everything on the sheet of paper ... It doesn't have to be beautiful ... the feeling will know what it means. Hesitantly Sophie starts with dark colors, then the stripes get stronger, the sobbing stops. She scratches with the crayon fiercely, adding more lines and another color. There is a deep sigh. Then there are yellow and orange circles. She looks up at her mother and smiles.

Sophie: It's gone.

Reflection:

• *What was your reaction to Sophie's crying? Do your recognize the adult tendency to say: "It wasn't so bad that those girls were standing there ... they weren't laughing at you ... they even helped you lift up your bicycle ... you shouldn't pay so much attention to what other children think."*

• *The crying is necessary until "it" is heard inside. If something is not heard, it remains hanging. When it is heard, it can be resolved.*

• *In this dialogue, Sophie's mother does not force her view of the situation on her daughter. Sophie was given the chance to draw on her own ability to govern herself.*

Learning to self-regulate feelings

Children can learn to be in control of their feelings. Once a young person becomes clear about what he really feels and wants, he can express himself in a controlled way. This can be done with or without language, but Focusing takes away the big struggle.

> *Jesse is an articulate 16-year-old. He is very angry because his teacher yelled at him and insulted him. He tells this story to his mentor.*
>
> *Jesse*: I was really scared. I could feel it through my whole body, like a kind of paralysis on the outside. Or like a skinned rabbit. While inside me it was boiling. I decided not to go to school the next day because I won't allow myself to be treated like this. That decision felt like a piece of steel plate inside. My mother was furious that I refused to go. I went to my room and stayed still with the feeling for a while. Then I started to draw and color. A lot of red came like a volcano erupting and bursting open. It was more anger than fear. I went through three or four sheets of paper. Slowly I felt my fear disappear and my anger lessen. The next day I did go to class. I felt a little tense, but also calm and sure of myself. The teacher didn't say anything and acted quite normally. I am going to pay a little more attention.

> ***Reflection***:
> *Can you imagine how Jesse's relationship with the teacher would have evolved if he hadn't calmed down? This adolescent notices peace and confidence because of his contact with his felt sense.*

Problems and feelings can be overwhelming for children. As adults, we sometimes succeed in putting things in perspective, but that is much more difficult for young people. With Focusing, however, they learn that the very fierceness of a feeling has meaning. As they listen to its inner story, they find resolution to problems without drowning in them.

Increasing concentration

Focusing can be especially helpful for children who have difficulty taking in new information. A learning block says something about the relationship between a child's inner experience and her ability to think. If the inner feeling is not clear, she cannot use her full capacity for thinking. Thus Focusing facilitates a child's concentration, as you saw in the fist example in this chapter, with Gonda and Kris.

Children get to know themselves better

When children make contact with the felt sense and symbolize it, they gain increased clarity. Focusing influences a child's self-image, as certain vague emotions become clear, and overwhelming problems are seen from a distance.

Susan is nine years old: Through drawing I have now put everything outside myself, and now I'm Susan again. My drunken father is on paper there and he is no longer inside. Now I'm just as normal again as the other children.

"I am drunk! And alcoholic"

FOCUSING AT DIFFERENT AGES

As you guide children along the way, there are some purposes and techniques suited to younger, and some to older children. Depending on the age you're working with, you'll want to emphasize different aspects of Focusing.

In this section we distinguish between babies (ages 0–2 years), toddlers (2–6 years), school-age children (6–12), and adolescents (12–16), and offer pointers for Focusing with each. Of course the categories are rough, and you should feel free to think outside of them, letting yourself be guided by the child's individuality.

Babies

Focusing can be introduced as soon as a baby is born or at any point that you as adult can reflect to the baby what you think it might be feeling. You can also instruct parents to observe their baby closely and give words to what they think is happening or what the baby might be thinking. Parents find that their babies are soothed when they attempt to verbalize how their baby might feel inside. (For more on this age group, see *Especially for Parents,* pp. 126–138.)

Children from 2 to 6

It is quite all right to invite preschoolers to focus. Children between the ages of two and six respond very naturally to the process. They are able to contact a felt sense and they act as experts on what they need.

At a day-care center, a caregiver may react to a child's tears with, "Shall we be nice to that sadness that Mommy and Daddy are leaving? Where is that sadness? What does it look like? Does it have a color? Would it be good to draw that on a sheet of paper?" Soon the child is so intensely involved in his drawing that he no longer needs to feel sad. With drawing, it fades away. It is especially helpful if the caregiver directs the child's attention to the felt sense. This process is different from the usual, "Come on, let's sit down and draw," which is often offered as a distraction away from the sadness, not a path to knowing it better.

To express the felt sense in words is difficult at this age. With colors and with the movement of their hands, child express their felt sense. You can help them by offering words for what you think might be going on inside them. But pay close attention to see whether or not your words are correct. Look particularly for non-verbal cues. Focusing with children at this age requires the utmost attention, as you may have to offer many guesses as to what is going on inside.

Cassie, well over two years old, is having a sleepover with her grandparents. At 6 o'clock she's tired but doesn't want to go to bed. She cries hard, saying: "I want my daddy. I want my mommy."

Her grandmother tries without success to comfort her. Then she changes her approach. She sits down on the floor beside Cassie with crayons and paper in her hand. Holding out the box of crayons, she asks: "What is the color of your sadness?" Cassie looks at the colors. Without hesitating, she takes the dark blue crayon. In a soft voice Granny repeats a few times: "You can feel all your sadness and sobs and tears inside ... and you can draw them on paper."

Cassie starts making horizontal lines back and forth in a flowing movement. Granny repeats that she can put all her sadness on paper by coloring. After a little while, the crying lessens and Cassie's voice changes. She says with anger: "I want my daddy. I want my mommy."

Granny says: "It seems as if something is angry inside you; can you draw that too?" With a strong hand Cassie makes vertical lines disconnected from each other. She lets out a deep sigh and says: "So." Then she gets up and starts to play.

Reflection:
Do you see how simple the symbolizing can be? Even though a girl of just two years old cannot yet put all her feelings into words, the Focusing process flows.

Children from 6 to 12
Children ages six to twelve are open to experiences that, like Focusing, have to do with who they are. The younger the children, the fewer the words you use. Simply demonstrate Focusing and let the children practice step by step. In time, they'll become familiar with the process. With older children you can offer more detailed explanations.

The following example shows how few words you need.

Jane, from New York, is familiar with Focusing and at age 10 is capable of directing her own process. As her companion, Marta has only to mirror Jane and suggest some next steps in the process. The change comes from inside Jane, from staying in touch with what she feels in her hands.

Marta: I invite you to go inside and notice what's asking for your attention.

Jane: My hand …

Marta: Your hand … one hand?

Jane shows her two hands with the palms up.

Marta: Two hands.

Jane holds out her right hand with the palm down.

Marta looks at it and says: This hand wants your attention …

Jane retracts her hand and closes her eyes.

Marta: Can you ask your hand what is the matter?

Jane nods with her eyes shut.

Marta: Something in your hand wants to express something.

Jane nods.

Marta: Does your hand know how it wants to express itself?

Jane nods yes. She looks for a crayon with her right hand and starts to sketch. She puts the crayon down and looks at her accompanier for a moment.

Marta: Oh, that comes from your hand.

Jane nods slowly.
Jane: Yes.
Marta: Does it have a story to tell?
Jane: Yes. *(She nods)*
Marta: Yes ... see if you want to tell it and
if your hand would be OK with that.
Jane nods yes.
Jane: First it moves in a circle.
Jane moves her right hand in a circle.
Marta mirrors what she says and does.
Marta: First it moves in a circle.
Jane rolls her hand around her wrist in a
circle. She places her hand on the sheet
of paper with her fingers spread out.
Marta: It makes a circle ... yes.
Jane: And then three fingers.
She shows three fingers on the paper.
Marta: Those are your three fingers.
Jane: They are there.

Marta: They are there. That is what your hand wants to express.
Jane: Yes.
Marta: Yes ... that is quite a story.
Jane: Yes.
Marta: Can you ask your hand whether it is finished?
Jane: Not completely yet.
Marta: Not yet ... there is more to come from your hand.
Jane looks in the tray for another crayon. For a minute and a
half she draws with her lower lip sucked in. Then she returns
the crayon to the tray.
Jane: My hand would really like to be a part of me.
Marta: Oh, your hand would really like to be a part of you ... so
   that it belongs to you.
Marta points with her finger to what Jane has just drawn. And
   now you drew that and does this drawing have something
   to tell you?
Jane: That's me... I'm running, very fast... and my hands are
   moving like this.
Jane moves her arms and legs.
Marta: And your hands are moving like this. *(Marta mirrors the*
   movement)
Jane nods and smiles.
Marta: And they want to be yours.
Jane nods and smiles at Marta, moving her upper body to and
fro.

Marta: *(Pointing to the drawing)* Here your hands are connected to your arms and connected to you.

Jane nods and smiles.

Marta: Can you feel that?

Jane: Yes.

Marta: Well, that is quite something. Can you ask your hands whether they are finished?

Jane: *(She closes her eyes for a second)* No.

Marta: No, there is more to come ...

Jane starts looking in the box of crayons and uses two crayons, one after another. She draws for a minute and a half and then looks at Marta.

Marta: That also belongs to your hand.

Jane: It likes writing ... especially my name and these are my initials ... and they are saying, "Here we are."

Marta: Oh yes ... your hand loves to write ... especially your initials. That is about you and it wants to say: here we are. That is quite something ... Here we are ... Does that feel good?

Jane nods and laughs.

Marta: Go and check whether they have finished or whether there is still more.

Jane: They have still more.

Jane looks for a crayon in the tray.

Marta: They have still more ... Is there enough room?

Jane nods and continues looking. First she draws with one crayon and then with three at a time. With pursed lips she draws for 30 seconds, looks at Marta for a second and speaks, while placing both her arms on her legs.

Jane: My hands deserve to be there.

Marta: Oh yes. They say they deserve to be there. It means that they are really important.

Jane nods and moves her arms and shoulders. She looks at Marta.

Jane: My hands don't have anything more to say now.

Marta: Your hands don't have anything more to say now. They are finished.

Jane: *(Nodding)* They deserve to be there.

Reflection:

• *Marta did not know that Jane had been struggling with writing. All the interventions Jane had received have been in vain. It was as though Jane felt her hands didn't belong to her. She wasn't able to make contact with them. It stands to reason, then, that writing was difficult for her. Now with her hands at her disposal, her writing can improve.*

• *Do you notice that as the companion you don't have to worry about the story of how Jane became alienated from her hands? The hands themselves receive attention. This enables them to effect a change: "Hey, we're part of you!"*

Adolescents from 12 to 16

Adolescents are engaged in a struggle to find their own identity. Making a connection with what's inside can be a real help to them in this process. A parent may not be the appropriate guide. You, as someone from outside the family, can be a real help to the adolescent since young people this age are usually in the process of detaching themselves from their parents.

A major appeal for adolescents is that in Focusing, privacy is respected. Privacy is exceptionally important to young people this age. Through Focusing, they can get to know themselves and their boundaries better. The Focusing companion teaches them the steps in Focusing and clearing a space and then gives them room to find their own way. This room is precisely what adolescents need at this stage of life: maximum control in learning to interact with their inner world. In Budapest, a group of five adolescents ages 14 to 18 meets once a month with a Focusing trainer. It is the young people themselves who ask to continue meeting. They report experiencing great support from the group.

You can teach adolescents to focus just as you would teach adults. The only difference is that with adolescents you include artistic and physical alternatives for symbolizing. With adolescents as with any group, the basic Focusing attitude of friendliness and openness remains important. (See *The Focusing Attitude,* pp. 95–101 for a more complete description.)

> *Thea, a social worker from a child welfare agency, has the difficult task of placing Sabrina, a fourteen-year-old, into foster care. Sabrina is furious. She refuses to cooperate. She curses, swears, and cries. Thea is an experienced focusing companion. She knows how important it is to stay with Sabrina and especially with what is going on inside her.*
> *Below are some of Thea's mirroring responses:*
>> Inside it does not feel at all right that I of all people am coming to take you to this other address.
>> There is a huge amount of anger inside you.
>> You would love to throw it all in my face.
>> It's as if the whole world is abandoning you.

Inside it really hurts that you can't stay at home.
Sabrina yells back:

It is totally black inside.

It's full of fire.

It's almost bursting inside.

The worst thing is that I won't be with my little brother
anymore.

Thea: Yes that is the very worst, that you won't be with your
little brother anymore.

*This makes Sabrina cry. Thea stays with Sabrina with all her
attention and understanding.*

Thea: That is really terrible for you, and you feel it inside.

*The terrible feeling inside Sabrina starts to fade away. Thea
gives her some space and promises to return the next day. The
next day Sabrina has calmed down. She says she understands
that she has to leave home and that it is for the best. Her
suitcase is packed.*

Reflection:

*Do you notice how calm Thea remains? She doesn't get
tense or afraid. She simply joins Sabrina where she is, and
from this, more space arises in Sabrina. It opens the way
for her to take the first step: noticing what is happening
inside her.*

3

Teaching Focusing
to the Individual Child

There are several ways to teach Focusing to children. You will make a conscious choice when to use each one, as there are marked differences between them.

- You can describe Focusing to one or more children in a general way.
- You can give them the experience of Focusing one on one, being their companion.
- You can teach the various steps separately, enabling them eventually to focus by themselves.
- You can teach them to "clear a space," which is useful and quick when there's a problem they need to set aside for the time being.

Whichever option you choose, you are the one who will make the offer to focus and accompany the child on the journey. You wait with friendly attention for what comes inside the child that is meaningful. and you sense how it is inside you too. This may be different from what you or the child is accustomed to. Focusing is not thinking, it is not wanting, it is not recalling the details of a situation. It is sensing the totality of experience.

DESCRIBING FOCUSING

Begin by asking the child's permission. Let her know a little about Focusing and ask whether she'd like to know more. In this way you avoid making a child feeling trapped, which makes them rebel instantly. It is better to knock on a figurative door and ask whether it is OK to come in.

After you have described Focusing a little, the child can ask questions, and you can describe the process some more. The number of questions you get will generally depend on the age and interest of the child. An adolescent will usually want more explanation than an eight-year-old.

How do you explain Focusing to an eight-year-old? You might read aloud all or part of the text below. Take your time so the child can absorb the words as you read them. Go slowly so that you yourself can experience the words as well. In this way you model a Focusing kind of attention, experiencing as you read. Feel free to choose the sentences and parts that fit. For some children you only have to use part of the text, for others you need to read it several times. Look and listen well for cues from the child as you are reading. Do you notice that they are following you?

When something nice happens you can feel that somewhere inside ...

Also when something unpleasant happens you feel that too somewhere in your body ...

Have you noticed that? Can you feel that? ...

We have good, warm, pleasant places inside ... and also difficult, troublesome things that get in our way or that don't feel right.

Have you ever noticed anything like that?

If you feel something heavy or pressing, it might feel as if things will never be OK again in your life ...

Then it is difficult to concentrate on your work ...

Sometimes you try really hard not to feel anything anymore ... not to let the feeling come out.

You push it down inside your body ... for instance, by swallowing your tears ... then you get such a tight, constricted throat ... or your stomach feels tense from holding it in ...

Does that sound familiar?

When we recognize this difficult feeling ... and we are friendly with it inside ... that can help us solve our problems ...

I do this and it helps me feel better ... there is more space ... and I can handle difficult things more easily.

I listen to those heavy difficult things inside me ... I ask if they have something to tell me ... sometimes a story ... there might be a picture ... a color ... or more colors ...

And you know ... the difficult things inside will disappear ... sometimes immediately ... sometimes gradually ...

Sometimes you already know which problem feeling needs attention ... it's itching so badly ... it's so heavy ... or dull ... you don't know yet what makes it so difficult ...

At other times you just have a feeling ... and you don't know what's really the matter ...

You just wait ... until something in your body makes it clear what the feeling is all about ... each feeling in your body has a story to tell ... and you slowly discover, "that's what it's about" ... or "that's what makes it so hard... or tight... or whatever it is " ...

It's a surprise that such a feeling and its message like to gently appear ... when we are quiet ... when we are nice to it ...
It doesn't matter what comes ... You can say "hello" to it nicely ... in the same way that you say "hello" to a nice friend ... then something unexpected happens ... something changes inside ... you can draw or color this problem ... or what has happened ... and what is coming up now ...
You know that it doesn't have to be a pretty drawing ...
Only whatever your hand wants to make on paper ...
Sometimes the feeling brings out only colored lines, circles or scratches ...
Inside, you know what it means ...

You will be able to look at your paper ... the paper on which you have drawn or colored your heavy problems or whatever you're feeling ... you will feel more space inside ... happier and calmer ... you can breathe more easily.
You find out that it is good to feel those troublesome feelings ... that is the way they can change and fade away ... now you are the boss in your body ... inside, you know what the right direction is ...

It's OK to tell me if I don't react correctly or if I say something that isn't right for you inside ... follow your own path ... always take the time to let something come up from inside ... you don't have to say anything or talk about it if it is private ... you can choose whether you want to focus with your eyes open or not ... sometimes your eyes close automatically after a little while because it helps you concentrate ...
You choose a calm safe place where it feels good to be ...
Would you like to do that with me?

These words are not a fixed text. They simply indicate a direction. Feel free to come up with your own adaptation that fits you, the child and the situation. Of course this description can be used with a group also, to give them some overview of Focusing.

BEING A CHILD'S COMPANION

A good time to offer Focusing is when the child is stuck with a problem. It works best when the child brings the problem to you.

Ask the child if it would be OK for you to work with the problem together in a new way. This invitation is of critical importance as it allows the child to take the first step towards his own inner knowing. Provide a short description, and then lead directly into a focusing experience.

Heinrich had a lot of experience with Focusing, but had never tried it with children. One day he sat down with Alex, his ten-year-old son. Heinrich tells this story.

> *My son Alex has problems with math. He is far behind his classmates.*
>
> *One day he refuses to go to school complaining about a stomachache. I want to help Alex look inside. I propose an experiment. I am not sure how I will do this, but I believe that what is good for me may be good for him too. I feel very clumsy. I intend to do a lot of mirroring.*
>
> *First I ask where he feels all that inside about his math. What comes up about it? He tells me that inside him it is a mess with dark, ugly faces. I ask him if he can stay with these faces or look at them from some distance. The faces are of the children who always bully him because he is stupid. He discovers that this is the worst part of it.*
>
> *Suddenly he tells me that butterflies are coming, more and more butterflies with beautiful colors. He smiles and says: "They are coming to help me ... They are saying that it's not so bad ... It feels much lighter now ... I will take the butterflies with me tomorrow."*
>
> *The next day Alex goes to school without any problem. Later he asks me to do that "hocus-pocus" again. He regularly asks me to do that "hocus-pocus" with a special tone in his voice.*

Reflection:

> • *What do you notice about Heinrich's basic attitude when accompanying his child? Do you notice that Heinrich realizes the importance of letting his son remain in control?*
> • *Alex's unique solution comes from inside him. Would you have thought of butterflies? The solution for Alex may not be right for any other child.*

You should not expect immediate results or such beautiful processes every time. You help the child most by allowing him to gain confidence in this way of working. Some children need time to familiarize themselves with Focusing. Other children are naturals; they focus as if they have never done anything else.

The less you expect from the child, the more space they will feel. And if they feel enough space, they'll come back for more.

An outline of the companion's steps

As the companion, you guide the children step-by-step in the beginning. Later, the steps flow together, change their order, and some get left out entirely.

The basic principle here is that something needs to go on with a child every moment. You encourage them to maintain their link between experiencing the problem they are focusing on, and the accompanying body sensations.

It is important to ask their permission at every step of the way. You never impose your interventions. The steps are not commands but suggestions, which they can take or leave. Your job is to create the time and space in which to be calm and attentive.

A red ball with blue lines:
"all fire in my belly"

The following brief summary of the Focusing steps for a child gives you a view of the Focusing process in its most extensive (complete?) form and lets you have all the options at your disposal. (See Appendix: *Protocols*, p.152, for a list of these steps and accompanying sentences.)

- create the conditions for Focusing
- let the child talk about the problem or question
- direct the child's attention inside
- help the child notice how he or she feels inside about the problem or question.
- suggest that the child stay with this bodily-felt sense
- encourage the child to draw or describe the inner story
- help the child notice the shift inside the body, stay in contact with it, and welcome it

We will clarify these seven steps using the following example of Esther being accompanied by her mother. A similar interaction could take place between Esther and her teacher. Note that the Focusing done by this 13-year old-girl is comparable to the Focusing process of an adult.

Creating conditions

Esther comes home from school with a gloomy and dejected face. She sits down at the kitchen table without saying a word. Esther's mother notices immediately that something is the matter, but it isn't always possible to delve into a problem right away. Esther is already used to Focusing with her mother, so her mother mirrors for a moment and then offers to focus with her later.

Mother: It seems as if something is not going well for you … Right now I don't have time to be with you … You could ask yourself if you want to deal with it at length this evening … if it would be alright if I were present … I am available this evening after eight o'clock … Just let me know. In the meantime you can maybe put it outside yourself by drawing it … Then it won't be in your way while you are doing your homework … Just see what feels good to you.

In this preliminary talk the conditions of time and place are established. Also at this time the adult asks permission: "May I accompany you in this difficult matter?" Asking this question confirms that the child is in control. Be sure to ask permission no matter how young the child is. When your child answers, pay attention not only to the words, but to the body language as well. You don't want to run the risk of ever violating a child's boundaries.

Let the child talk about the problem or question

When Esther's mother has time, she and her daughter sit down together in a comfortable spot. Esther's mother invites her to share briefly the heart of the problem.

Mother: Can you tell me in two sentences what it's all about? … As you know, it's not necessary to say anything out loud as long as you have a clear sense of it inside.

Esther: Today Eva suddenly went off with that new girl and left me alone.

It is helpful to ask a child to share the problem in just two sentences. You don't want spend too much time on the story line, because just talking won't get you anywhere. No matter what comes, you mirror it.

Direct the child's attention inside

Unlike adults, most children are readily able to direct their attention inward. You don't have to sit down solemnly and lead their attention there. However, if the child likes it, you can use the following sentences.

> *Mother*: Be aware that your feet are on the ground ... if you wiggle your toes you can feel them better ... Can you feel your body sitting in the chair and touching the back of the chair and the seat? Can you feel your hands? If not, move them a little ... Can you feel your breathing going in and out? Now let your attention sink inside ... if you want to, you can close your eyes ... When you are ready to go on, wave your hand to let me know.

With this last remark the Focusing companion affirms that she is willing to follow Esther's pace. She invites Esther to close her eyes, but does not instruct her to do so. Children and young people often focus with their eyes open. Whether or not they close their eyes may have to do with how secure they feel.

How does the child feel inside about the problem or the question?

> *Mother*: Now imagine again what happened today...
>
> *Esther*: Today Eva went off with that new girl and left me in the lurch and I was all alone during recess.
>
> *Mother*: *(after mirroring: see p. 39)* Check where in your body you feel that, now that you recall it.
>
> *Esther*: It's here, mainly near my heart.
>
> *She points to it with a clenched right hand, like a fist against her chest. Her mother mirrors her words and gesture.*
>
> *Mother*: Now take your time to check how it feels there in your body ...
>
> *Esther*: Very solid ... hard ...

Stay with the bodily sense

> *Mother*: Very solid ... hard ... Can you be friendly with it? Can you stay with it, giving it your full attention?
>
> *Esther*: It's as hard as a boulder ... a very heavy boulder.

For Esther the felt sense is "as hard as a very heavy boulder." Most children can easily point out the physical sensations in their body as they describe their felt sense. Esther perceives it near her heart.

Draw or describe the inner story

> *Mother*: As hard as a heavy boulder ... Check whether this is exactly right. The felt sense near your heart and that phrase

'very heavy boulder' … maybe it still has something more to tell you.

Esther: That boulder can't roll. Today I was as heavy as a boulder that can't roll … and that is a good thing really … they couldn't just push me aside

There is a long silence after mother's mirroring.

Esther: But then I couldn't walk over to the other group of girls either …

Another long silence follows mother's mirroring.

Esther: It was more that I thought Eva had decided all of a sudden that I was stupid and that really scared me … as if I couldn't move any more …

Esther's mother mirrors the inner steps that are developing. She doesn't have to do anything else. She is careful not to interrupt the silences because Esther is clearly in contact with her felt sense of the problem.

Notice the shift inside the body, stay in contact with it, and welcome it

Esther: It is getting much softer now inside near my heart … the boulder is getting smaller and smaller … my heart is starting to feel free again …

Mother mirrors the words.

Esther: I am going to spend some time with the other kids tomorrow … they're nice too … maybe they'll let me join in.

Mother: *(after mirroring: see below)* Do you notice that sigh? How does it feel inside now?

Esther: Very different, and I know how I'm going to act tomorrow.

Mother: Can you stay with that with friendly attention and just receive it?

Esther has found a clear action step. This may not always be the case, especially when a child uses a non-verbal form of symbolizing. A felt shift in and of itself is already a sufficient result.

Being with it, listening and mirroring

Communication between you and the child is always improved if you mirror his or her words. It shows your caring attention. This is the starting point for accompanying the child on his inner journey. The safety of knowing you are there, and the surety of being heard that mirroring gives, help the child go deeper inside himself. The child can make a connection with what is really going on inside. With your presence you give the child the necessary confidence to develop her own process.

Watch the child for signals that your mirroring resonates or misses the mark. Luckily, if you say something that doesn't match his felt sense, the child will usually let you know. Don't take it personally, just drop that suggestion and go on.

Notice the difference between "Can you tell me what it is saying inside?" and "What is it saying inside?" The first sentence places you in a central position, as someone who needs to know. The second sentence keeps the child's concentration on himself and his felt sense. As much as possible, keep the words, "I" and "me" out of it.

The child's problem may not disappear, but he will see that it needn't get in the way of everything he tries to do. He will feel new freedom in his body.

COMPLETE EXAMPLE

The next situation is completely different. Instead of Focusing between mother and daughter, the setting concerns a therapist and a five-year-old child. However, the process is remarkably similar. This example also shows how easy the process can be, even if the material is difficult, because the child takes the necessary steps himself. Notice how the therapist accompanies him, mirroring and inviting the child to symbolize what he discovers inside.

> *Jens is five. A few months ago, his grandmother burned before his eyes in a house fire. She lay in a coma in the hospital for a few weeks and then she died. Jens did not go to the funeral and has been having nightmares ever since. His parents have brought him to see Erik, a psychologist. In his first session with Erik, Jens reports that he is afraid of fire. At the start of their second session, Erik mirrors this.*

Erik: Something inside you is afraid of fire.
Jens: There is fire at Granny's house.
Erik: Do you want to draw something about it? How all that is inside you?
Jens: *(drawing)* The house is on fire ... the fire is crashing against Granny.
Erik: The fire is crashing against Granny.
Jens: Crashes against Granny.
*He makes his drawing (**A**) using several different colors. Then he looks up, lost in thought.*
Jens: I still need to add curls to the hair.

A

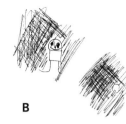

B

C

He puts this drawing in front of the therapist and immediately starts on a second drawing. He draws a brown surface with a flower in it (**B**).

Jens: There is a little mud outside with a flower.

Erik: A little mud with a flower ...

Jens: And then Jens is added to it.

He draws a second plot of mud, this one with a boy "Jens" in it. (**B**).

Jens: I was afraid.

After this he lets out a deep sigh.

Erik: Wow, that fear comes out of a deep place inside your body, such a deep sigh.

Jens: I walked really fast away from the house.

Next Jens draws a house, far away from himself and the flower (**C**).

Erik: You were afraid that this house would catch fire.

Jens: The floor caught fire, but Granddad put it out.

Before the psychologist can say anything, Jens takes out another sheet of paper.

Jens: I want to make another drawing. *Draws* (**D**). *Granny is dead. Jens draws his grandmother with her curls. Next to that he draws a rectangle* (**D**).

Jens: She is put in a cabinet.

Erik: She is put in a box.

Jens: *(reacting quickly)* In a cabinet.

The therapist mirrors this without knowing what "cabinet" means exactly. Afterwards he finds out that the grandmother was cremated and that her ashes are kept in a cabinet. Next, Hans draws five faces (**D**).

Jens: We are sad because granny is dead ... The smallest one is Diederik, my twin brother ... I am also there.

Erik mirrors that everyone is sad. Jens looks at the drawing for another second, and then takes a new sheet of paper.

D

Jens: Aunt Clara died normally and I want to draw her too.

He draws Aunt Clara (**E**).

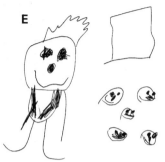

E

Jens: I drew them all looking sad.

Erik: Everyone is sad: Jens, Diederik Aunt Clara, Mommy and Daddy.

Jens doesn't react. The psychologist wants to put the drawing materials aside, but Jens does not.

Jens: I want to draw something else.

He starts to draw. Granny and auntie each with their own cabinet (F).

Jens lets out a deep sigh as he draws the cabinet (F).

Erik: A sigh from deep within your body.

Jens steps away from the table.

Jens: Now I want to play.

F

A week later Jens' parents come for a consultation. The therapist is surprised when they show him some drawings Jens drew in school. They are the same drawings! It seems that the teacher wanted to light a few candles around Christmas time, but she noticed that fire made Jens anxious. She knew what had happened to his grandmother and she took the time to listen to Jens. Jens started to draw in her presence and went through exactly the same process as the week before with the therapist, ending with a picture of his grandmother and his aunt with their cabinets. At the end of class, Jens blew out a candle.

Reflection:

• *Do you notice how Jens himself is in control of the process? All the therapist and teacher had to do was to be there and to mirror now and then.*

• *When the therapist gives back the word "box" instead of "cabinet," Jens corrects him very quickly. As the companion you accept any correction, even if you don't know what it means. When you are open to corrections from the child, you don't need to be afraid of making serious mistakes while mirroring.*

4

Teaching Focusing to Groups

In order to teach children to focus on their own, you emphasize intermediary steps, each of which can be practiced separately. This teaching can easily take place in a group, so it is a useful tool in the classroom, where individual attention is more difficult to give. You can build up a program that extends from six to ten weeks; the longer time is ideal for teaching the teachers as well, who then can extend the program over the entire school year.

You will see that when a group of teachers and children knows how to focus, a different atmosphere develops at school or in the institution. Another advantage of teaching children the individual steps is that they can make use of them independently, that is, they can continue to do Focusing at home.

Once again you unravel the Focusing process into separate parts. This makes teaching it more orderly and manageable. But you need to remember that the actual process is not always one of clear steps. In the outline are many possibilities. You will make a choice from among them and decide what is best at any given moment.

The exercises we describe were created for children between the ages of six and twelve, but they work well for other age groups, taking into account the age differences described in Chapter 2. Feel free to adapt as you sense what the best step would be.

As always when introducing Focusing, you need to give an explanation each time about what you are going to do and why. Never spring an exercise on children without this preamble. Always invite them in a friendly way to take this journey with you. As you continue, observe the individual reactions of the children all the time and take your cues from them. And finally, clearly guard your time limits; there will always be a next time.

AN OUTLINE OF THE LEARNING STEPS

The following section describes steps which lead the group from something familiar, developing sensory awareness in their bodies (A), to the less familiar, turning attention inside (B). It proceeds to teach the children how to be friendly to what comes up inside (the felt sense) (C), and how to create a safe space (D). These activities empower the children to deal with any heavy, difficult felt sense that might arise in the future.

The next two steps (E and F) deal with images that children invent or imagine and only later will the children deal with actual events that they live through. Children often discover the felt sense first with the aid of their imagination and only later make the link to daily life. The children first use their imagination to discover a felt sense (E), and then verbalize or draw the felt sense which they have discovered in this way (F). Next, the children progress, first, to linking pleasant experiences to the felt sense (G), and then doing the same with difficult experiences (H). They are encouraged to stay with the felt sense long enough so that their inner sense can unfold and shift (I). Finally the shift is received and acknowleged, and even symbolized, so that the new feeling will grow (J).

Preparation

When children are very young, Focusing happens easily. Young children love to focus and for them it is natural. It is more difficult when you start it at a later age and children are not used to Focusing. You present something new and children may react, "Don't come to me with that stuff."

You need all your enthusiasm, because children quickly experience this teaching as obtrusive. Take your time and let them become curious about what is coming. Avoid their resistance by offering that which is new in very small steps. Wait patiently until the children ask for more. Time and again it is a matter of finding a good balance between distance and closeness. Don't keep after the children, but stay close, providing every opportunity.

Just as with individual Focusing, it is best to have a safe place where children will not be disturbed. Let them find their own space by moving the tables and chairs. Teachers say that children often continue to move the desks around each time in order to create a safe place. One teacher puts a carpet down in the middle of the classroom, with pillows around it and the children sit on the pillows. Another teacher has the library of the school at his disposal; it is extra quiet there. This peace and quiet are essential during Focusing. It may be a good idea to put a "Do no disturb" sign on the door.

If you use the classroom it is necessary to make a clear difference between the moment of Focusing and the moment of academic learning. This can be done by hanging up a banner or by writing "listening to each other" on the blackboard. One teacher always begins by writing: "listening inside" on the blackboard in elegant letters. She notices that the children react enthusiastically, as if it's their favorite activity of the week. Another teacher hangs a large drawing with the word "I" on it just inside the classroom door.

An important point in preparation is that you make a connection with your own inner depth. Then your attitude and voice will create the right atmosphere.

THE LEARNING STEPS IN A COMPLETE GROUP PROGRAM

A. Developing sensory awareness in the body

In the following exercise, the children get used to noticing their bodies. They begin to make contact with how they feel inside. This contact influences and improves their bodily self-image. You can offer these exercises as a way to relax between lessons, as you introduce children to the practice. Or you can use them to help their attention go inside at the beginning of a longer Focusing session.

Each time, a few children will react with real enjoyment. These few will stimulate the other children to enjoy what is happening. You will notice that these exercises make an appeal to movement and the senses: smell, touch, hearing, sight, and taste. You will become creative in making up more exercises yourself. (Do not offer all of the following exercises at the same time. They are also all included in the Appendix: *Protocols*, pp. 153–158.

> *Stamp with your feet ... then put your hand to your heart and feel how it is beating ...*
>
> *Pull your shoulders up as high as you can ... up to your cheeks ... How does that feel? How deep do you feel that in your body? Now let your shoulders drop ... Do you notice the difference?*
>
> *Clench your fists ... feel what happens in your body.*
>
> *Clench your teeth ... What do you feel? How does that feel? Where else in your body do you feel it?*
>
> *What happens in your body when you imagine swinging high on a swing?*
>
> *Gently stroke the upper side of your arm with the tips of your fingers ... now stroke the underside ... Do you notice the difference?*
>
> *Now, without hurting yourself, scratch your arm on top ... now scratch the underside ... do you notice a difference? Can you feel a difference inside your body ... your belly or your chest?*
>
> *Listen to your breathing ... Put your hand on your belly and feel*

how it goes up and down.

*What happens inside when you imagine biting into a slice of
   lemon ... and now into something sweet ... do you notice
   the difference in your body?*

*Listen attentively to everything you hear when you open your
   ears ... Feel what happens inside you.*

*Look at this image with a little star ... this nice plant ... these
   flowers ... Notice that there is more and more that you are
   noticing ... What is happening inside now?*

Children like this type of exercise. Invite them to invent more exercises
that bring attention to what's inside their bodies. How much can
they become aware of?

B. Turning the attention inside

Children need to feel safe before they can allow their attention to go
inward. You can help create a safe place by providing clarity about
the time frame. Make an appointment with the children: check with
yourself how much time you have for Focusing and communicate
this to the children. Let them know how long the experience will
take. Focusing with children need not take up a lot of time.

Invite the children to sit in a relaxed way. In a class in Japan the
children simply lay their heads on their desks. This has the advantage
that there is less distraction. In time, their concentration will grow
deeper and they no longer distract each other.

The following sentences can help children turn their attention
inside. Be sure to give them enough time. By paying attention to the
children's reactions you can adjust the pace. It will also help if you
go inside yourself with your attention. In the beginning you will search
for the right pace, but just make sure that you don't go too fast.

Can you feel both your feet on the floor?

*Sometimes it helps when you wiggle your toes, that way you
   can feel them better ...*

*Feel that your body is sitting in the chair ... can you feel your
   back touching the seat?*

*Can you feel where your hands are? If not, move them a little
   ...*

Feel your shoulders ...

Feel how your breath goes in and out ...

If you want you can close your eyes ...

Now let your attention sink inside ...

Sense what it feels like in your chest and stomach area ...

Say a nice friendly hello to those feelings inside ...

Children often turn their attention inside with their eyes open. You don't need to insist that they close their eyes.

C. Being friendly to what comes (or tracking a problem)

You can teach children that there is a new, friendly way of dealing with unpleasant feelings. One third-grade teacher (children aged between 7 and 9) starts her class off this way:

> *What happens to you when something bad occurs and that bad thing is in the way? Is your first reaction just like mine? We don't want that feeling in our body at all ...*
>
> *We try to push it away ... to forget it by doing other things ... maybe even naughty things ... You might think that other children are bad or stupid ... Then an angry feeling forms inside ... We feel cheated ... resentful ... disappointed. Everything gets stuck inside ... It becomes harder and harder not to feel bad ... how do we get out of this?*
>
> *Shall we do something different about it today? Has anyone found such a spot inside already? Where an angry feeling is located ... where it is stuck? Who has already experienced something like that?*

The teacher allows all the children who want to say something to do so, and she mirrors their reactions.

> *Now we let our attention sink back inside. As we practice, this will become easier and easier to do.*

The teacher repeats the sentences about bringing the attention inside.

> *Now say to yourself: "Hello, nice child"..."Hello ..." and then softly say your name. Feel what happens inside ... Does anything change?*
>
> *Inside yourself you search for something that is angry or sad. You search for where there is something in the way ... Now you say something nice to it. Like: "I know that you're inside there grumbling ... I know that you're angry or sad or tired ... I am coming to sit with you and will wrap my arms around you ..."*
>
> *Do you notice anything changing in your feelings inside now? Take the time to draw that changed feeling ... give it a color ... Your hand knows how it wants to draw ...*

The teacher ends this part with a short discussion in which the children recount their experiences if they desire. Note that this Focusing step — where the child is friendly to whatever problem is inside — can also be used when there are difficulties with academic learning.

D. Creating a safe place

After receiving what comes in a friendly way, you can teach the children to create a safe place. Below are a few examples:

> *Imagine that you have your favorite soft toy in your arms. How does it feel to hold it? If something difficult comes ... something that needs your attention ... make an extra strong connection between you and your toy ...*
>
> *What is a safe color ... a color that helps you ... which color makes you feel protected? Take that color in your mind and bring it to something difficult ... You can draw with this color on your sheet of paper before you draw that difficult thing ... Or let the total feeling of that color come into your body ... How does it feel inside now?*
>
> *Imagine that there's a very safe place ... a place that you can see before you now ... you know that it's good and safe there ... like your inside wants this ... It does not have to be a real place ... it can be a place created by your imagination ... Sometimes it helps to draw that safe place so that you can call it up in your imagination more easily ... Can you feel the safe feeling of that place in your body?*

A safe place

Keep reminding the children to be friendly and patient with what comes up in their bodies. Help them learn to ask themselves how they feel inside. Encourage the children to stay with their feelings even if they seem vague or soft or unclear in the beginning.

The children learn to make use of a safe place. They learn to create a warm climate in themselves to approach their difficult experiences. Through this they develop more self-confidence.

E. Using the imagination to discover a felt sense, and staying with it

In this step, you help the children to discover a felt sense for daily occurrences, experiences, memories and images. Children find this very natural and enjoy putting it into words. They develop a new language for speaking about themselves and their bodily experiences. Explain to the children in your group that felt senses often have important stories to tell. Offer some examples to give them an idea of what you mean:

> *Walk as if you were a giant ... Where do you feel that inside? And how does that feel?*
>
> *Walk like a elf ... Where do you notice that inside? What is different?*
>
> *Stand like a tree ... How do you notice that inside? Where is that feeling located?*
>
> *How would you feel inside if you had your favorite cuddly toy with you now? Where is that feeling located?*
>
> *Imagine something hard ... Check what you feel inside ... now imagine something soft ... does the feeling change?*
>
> *Think of someone who is very sweet ... How does that make you feel?*
>
> *What do you notice inside when you succeed at something that seemed difficult at first?*

You can of course make up more of this type of exercise yourself.

F. Expressing and drawing the felt sense via the imagination

Let the children get used to the fact that the felt sense can be expressed in symbols. As we have seen, an image or drawing can come directly from the feeling inside. The feeling of change, or a "shift" in the body, lets you know when that image is exactly right.

After leading the children to discover their felt sense, ask them which colors would best represent it. Which movement does the hand want to make? In this way you help the children symbolize what they feel inside. And as they symbolize it, the feeling changes.

For this step you will of course need material: paper, colored pencils, pastel crayons or paint. Paint in particular can be very expressive. (See Chapter 10: *Symbols*, pp. 102–114) Wait to distribute the material until after the children have let their attention go inside. After a little while, invite the children to open their eyes and draw. At first some children will wait obediently with their eyes shut. You can encourage them, saying:

This is not a drawing like the ones you normally create. It doesn't have to be a pretty drawing. You don't need an eraser. Inside you, it knows what your drawing means. You can also use the other side of the paper or take a new sheet of paper. If you have closed your eyes, you can open them while you draw. Sometimes something comes that doesn't want to be put on paper. A white sheet of paper can also have a whole story to tell.

Let the children use the following imagined scene to evoke a felt sense. Take your time with these instructions. If you move too quickly, children will lose contact with what they're noticing inside.

Imagine that you're on the beach ... or in the woods ... or in some other nice place ... Pick one location ... it's OK if it's an imaginary place ... What comes up in your body ... for instance in your belly or in your chest?

When you notice a feeling ... take your time to stay with it... Does a word or image come? ... something that's just like that place, something that belongs to it? Write or draw what you feel inside ... including what has just come up ... You know it does not have to be a beautiful drawing... Sometimes a color or various colors come ...

For some children the beach or the woods are enjoyable places, but you can introduce other possibilities:
- listening to favorite music
- playing with a best friend

"Yippee, Yippee"
Lying in bed at night

G. Linking pleasant experiences to the felt sense
The previous two steps take place at the level of the imagination: the children imagine that they have their cuddly toy with them, or that they are gnomes. The next step is for them to make a connection with their daily experiences. Teach them there is another step beyond

using their imaginative powers. The children know now that they can feel everything they experience in their bodies, so this is not a hard step for them.

At first, have the children practice symbolizing or drawing feelings which are pleasant. Learning to focus is more long lasting when there is also attention to good feelings inside. Be prepared, though, for difficult feelings if they come up. Children may recall bad memories, nightmares, or a feeling of being abandoned. Encourage the children to stay also with these feelings, drawing them until they feel something shift.

> *You:* Have you experienced something fun recently?
>
> *(The children react)* My mother's birthday ... the amusement park ... my kitten ... I played with my best friend ...
>
> *You*: Think about it again now ... Imagine that you are experiencing it again and how nice it was ... Let it get calm inside ... Feel that nice feeling in your body ... Where in your body do you notice it?
>
> *You*: Check if this is easier to do with your eyes shut ... now let it become very calm inside ...

Here the teacher may give a sensory exercise, directing the attention inward.

> *Now let's listen inside and say to that feeling: "Hello, it is nice that you are there."*
>
> *Can you feel that nice feeling in your body even better now? ... Where in your body do you notice it?*
>
> *If something comes, wait to feel what it's really like there ... What word or color or image goes with it? No matter what comes up inside you, it's OK ... You keep feeling what there is. Then you can write or draw or color it on your paper ... Then you'll be able to look at it ... and this nice feeling will stay and even grow.*

H. Linking difficult experiences to the felt sense

Of course, besides feeling nice and comfortable, children can feel difficult feelings inside their bodies. They also make contact with what is in the way of being happy. Drawing is powerful, especially when more than one feeling arises, because the child can look at the whole of it. Children report that this gives them a new space inside.

The first time you explain this process, follow some of the suggestions below and wait for the children to react.

Everyone has difficult, unpleasant things inside sometimes ... something that bothers them ... something in your life that doesn't feel good ... You can feel it in your body ... notice what happens inside when you think about it ... be friendly to what is there ... it can helps you solve your problem.
I do this and it helps me feel better.
Giving attention to these feelings and drawing them helps to make them smaller and lets them change ... If you feel something heavy or piercing or pinching in your body ... it might feel as if you'll never feel good again ... that makes it hard to listen to your teacher ... hard to concentrate on your work ...

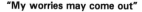

"My worries may come out"

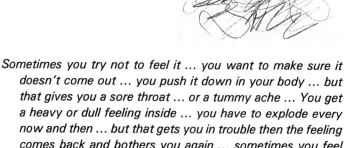

Sometimes you try not to feel it ... you want to make sure it doesn't come out ... you push it down in your body ... but that gives you a sore throat ... or a tummy ache ... You get a heavy or dull feeling inside ... you have to explode every now and then ... but that gets you in trouble then the feeling comes back and bothers you again ... sometimes you feel that you don't understand yourself anymore ... and no one who understands you ... Have you ever felt something like this?
Now we are going to gives some attention to any heavy, difficult feelings inside ... If you listen to it in a friendly way you will find out that slowly, slowly, as you draw it, the feeling becomes different ...
Sometimes you know right away what the problem is ... you know what in your life is connected to the heavy, dull feeling ... At other times you just have the feeling and you don't know what it's about ...
You just wait patiently ... you listen inside your body ... and wait until something comes, some sense of what it's all about ... because that feeling in your body has a story to tell ... gradually your body will discover: "That's what it's all about!" ...
These feelings and stories come up very gently if you're calm

and friendly to them ... if you stay friendly to everything that comes ... You can say "hello" to it nicely as you would to yourself or to a good friend ...

You can draw this problem or this difficult situation ... it doesn't have to be a beautiful drawing ... draw it exactly like your inside feeling wants to make it ... Sometimes the feeling brings colored lines, circles or scratches ... When you draw unpleasant, heavy, difficult feelings you will find that they change inside ... You get the chance to look at them ... You can feel easier and calmer ... you can breathe better ... You discover that it's good to give attention to those difficult feelings.

I. Staying with the felt sense so it can unfold

When adults focus, they "resonate" between the felt sense and the handle word or image, in order to deepen and unfold the process. In children the felt sense deepens as they draw. You instruct children to stay with the felt sense as they work.

Calmly review your paper every now and then ... What has come? Does it fit your feeling inside exactly? Sometimes there is even more to come ... Take time for that.

You will notice that the process carries itself forward. Sonya, a nine-year-old girl, experienced something she called "the black." Here's how she worked her way through it:

The teacher is observing Sonya as she colors a light green background on her paper. She lightly adds different colored circles, moving from the outside to the inside. From one corner fierce black lines appear unexpectedly, in a kind of triangle. Around that she makes black dots and finally a red circle enclosing the black.

She puts the paper aside and draws the same thing again, only this time the black lines are more vague and much bigger. Sonya tells the teacher, "It's OK for the black to leave now."

Reflection:

You can imagine that Sonya is expressing something black inside herself. By putting it on paper something changes for her inside. "It's OK for the black to leave now" sounds like a relief. The black thing which was at first so dark is liberated. This is called a felt shift.

J. Receiving the shift

When a shift is felt inside, it is important that the child recognize it, hold on to it and reinforce it. Then the shift will manifest itself more in future behavior.

> *Do you feel what it's like to have more feeling of space ... power ... freedom ... or whatever the new feeling is inside you? Where is it in your body? What does it feel like there? Does the new feeling have a color or an image? Perhaps it wants to be expressed on paper too ... Go ahead and draw it now, to reinforce that new feeling and make it even stronger ...*

5

Important Refinements

After you have read the previous two chapters on teaching Focusing to groups and individuals, you will find there are several useful refinements to the teaching process. "Clearing a space" is a useful Focusing tool which can be applied to either individual or group instruction. Teaching mirroring will be useful for your group sessions. And finally, you will want to decide how to deal with each and every child's drawing.

CLEARING A SPACE

"Clearing a space" is a way to begin a Focusing session, or it can be a separate and complete process. In "clearing a space" children don't delve deeply into the feelings inside. Rather they process them lightly and learn how to put them aside. It helps children to free themselves at that moment from the problems they might be carrying.

A school day requires a lot of concentration. Children are asked to sit still for hours, while all sorts of things might be going on inside them. There are so many minor and major problems, unrelated to schoolwork, that children deal with. It wastes their mental energy to drag these around all day.

Children can use their great power of imagination to clear a space for themselves, thereby freeing up some energy. "Clearing a space" involves bringing out, one by one, each of the things that is troubling them and stowing them in an imaginary safe place. Drawing makes this process more concrete, and helps open a spacious feeling inside. A child is able to experience who he or she really is, when the excess baggage is put down for a moment.

"Future"
"Which school later on?"
"How will I go to work"
"Sitting alone"
"Concentration!!"

Can you imagine how making a list like the above example helps a child feel better, less burdened? Afterwards, teachers report, the children occupy themselves more freely with other tasks.

"Clearing a space" can be completed entirely in the imagination, but making a picture is much more powerful for children. Use pencils, crayons, or ballpoint pens if you don't have much time. Drawing a face or body shape helps the child locate all the felt senses.

Clearing a space, step by step

"Clearing a space" consists of asking the children five questions:
- What's in the way of your feeling fine?
- Where do you feel it and how does it feel?
- What kind of images or words belong with it?
- Can you put it an imaginary safe place or express it on paper?
- How does it feel now?

You repeat these questions until everyone feels clear inside.

Here is the full version. After the children are quiet and ready, ask the children to say to themselves ...

> *Hello nice child ... Maybe you have a problem or something difficult that you have experienced today ... yesterday ... or something that's going to come tomorrow ... something that's bothering you right now ...*
>
> *Check where you feel that in your body ... Maybe you have a sad feeling ... an angry feeling ... a scared feeling ... maybe somewhere your body feels compressed ... pierced ... or dull ...*
>
> *Notice how it is with you in your body.*
>
> *Where do you feel that? How does that feel inside? Imagine putting this feeling at a little distance away from you, in some comfortable spot. Maybe there's a color or image that goes along with it. Take your time and draw it on paper ... open your eyes now ... When you've drawn it, that difficult thing is on your sheet of paper instead of inside you ...*
>
> *Now go back to that place inside your body, where it was ... Does it feel different in there now?*
>
> *Often there is more than one thing that is bothering you ... Take some time to feel again inside ... If you want to, you can close your eyes ... Something else may come up that is in the way of your feeling fine ... Sometimes it is an unpleasant, difficult feeling ... You might not even know what it is about ...*
>
> *Wait and see if a color goes with it ... Does that feeling have a*

color or shape? Let your hand move over the paper with your pencil or crayon ... let it move in a way that goes with the feeling ... so that the feeling itself comes out on the paper ...

Check and see if you feel more room inside ... Go back inside a few more times to see if there is still more that wants to come out on paper ...

Each time notice the lovely feeling of spaciousness in there ... You can draw that too ... Maybe you want use a fresh sheet of paper ... Maybe it has a word or an image ... As you draw, the space becomes even stronger so that you can hold onto it better.

In clearing a space children do not spend a long time with any one feeling or problem. The idea is to put difficult feelings aside temporarily until the moment when they can spend a longer time with Focusing. Clearing a space is used when you *don't* have much time!

Iona is a speech therapist at a Romanian school for children with multiple handicaps. She also takes care of children who are disruptive in the classroom. That's why Iona is called to help with Nicholas. He is lying on the floor, screaming through everything. Twelve-year-old Nicholas has grown up with a serious physical handicap and a slight mental retardation. Open and receptive, Iona goes and sits with him on the floor. She takes her time. There are sheets of paper and pastels nearby.

Iona: You are screaming.

Nicholas: (in a loud screaming voice) I don't want to do math ... I don't want to do anything!

Iona: You don't want to do anything, including math ... Is it here?

She puts her hand on her chest and makes an inviting gesture to Nicholas. Nicholas moves his own hand over his chest and lets his hand rest near his stomach.

Nicholas: Here.

Iona: Can you be friendly inside to that screaming?

Nicholas brushes his hand across his stomach.

Iona: Does this screaming have a color inside?

Nicholas takes a red pastel. Iona makes a scratching gesture.

Iona: The screaming moves from inside to outside, onto the sheet of paper ...

Nicholas starts making short powerful scratches everywhere on the sheet of paper.

Iona: ... until all the not wanting and the screaming is out.

Nicholas continues with black. Then green and yellow are added until he lays down the pastel with a sigh.
Iona: You seem like an emptied balloon.
Nicholas starts to laugh. A few minutes later he goes back to his class.

Reflection:
• *Do you notice how quickly clearing a space can work? It is a micro-process, but it is very powerful.*
• *Nicholas' teacher wants Iona to teach her how to clear a space as soon as possible. She sees what a good effect it has in a very short time.*

The effect of clearing a space

Children who are familiar with clearing a space find pleasure in their activities more quickly. When confronted with difficult problems, they know how to place them outside themselves. They advise each other to paint or draw something that is bothering them. Teachers often observe that children find clearing a space important. This micro-process not only influences the moment itself, but continues to be felt over time.

Clearing a space is used as a way to distance anyone from anything burdensome that stands in the way of free functioning and concentration. You can use it briefly for yourself if you are having a hard day. You use it to help the children — as a group or individually — feel fully present in the classroom. As it happens, clearing a space isn't only for unpleasant things. Something exciting like a birthday party can also hinder concentration. Putting something exciting to one side will also give the children more attention for learning.

TEACHING CHILDREN TO MIRROR EACH OTHER

To "mirror" is to reflect back the words or meaning of the speaker, or to repeat the gist of what a person is saying. To mirror someone shows that you are listening. (For more on listening and mirroring, see Chapter 8, pp. 83–94.) For many children, listening only means silently waiting for a turn. This can be difficult for them, since children are naturally active. Focusing gives you an opportunity to redefine listening, showing just how important, and even active it can be. Children need to be about eight before they can learn to mirror each other. In a small group, seven-year-olds can learn as well.

After you have modeled some mirroring, explain what people use it for:
• to check if the listener understood what is said

- to help the speaker hear her own words again and maybe understand them better
- to slow the speaker down so the listener can absorb what is being said
- to provide support when sad feelings come
- to provide support and even intensify happy feelings

As the first step in teaching mirroring, divide the children into pairs. In each twosome, one child will tell a story and the other will listen. Show them how to repeat each other's sentences. After three minutes, have them switch roles.

The children can also practice mirroring during group discussions, where you have more control over the situation. You pair up children who sit opposite each other, not next to each other. In this way the group discussion becomes more interesting and exciting.

It also works well to link the practice of mirroring to Focusing time. Children can mirror each other as they clear a space or after a Focusing experience. In pairs, they can describe the drawings that symbolize their experience and their partners can mirror this.

Mirroring is a welcome tool during all disagreements and quarrels. It helps children understand each other's perspective. Children also appreciate the chance to mirror some of what you say, especially when it's part of decision-making or disagreements. It's especially encouraging when you and the children dare to express what is going on inside you. Try it!

Teaching tips
There are a few general items to consider when teaching Focusing. First, it is important to be clear to the children how you will handle their drawings. Second, ending the focusing process requires some special care. You must be sure to leave time for discussion. Finally, a number of problems can crop up: sometimes children disturb each other, sometimes children don't want to participate. Once again you deal with this behavior carefully because it could carry important meaning. You give that individual some gentle attention.

A. Preserving children's drawings
In some classes children keep Focusing notebooks. They draw in these notebooks every time, both in a group and individually. The children keep the notebooks themselves, which takes care of confidentiality. They leave them at school and turn to them whenever they want to.

In other groups the children draw on loose-leaf paper. At the end of a focusing session, the teacher collects the drawings and places them in the children's personal folders. If a child does not want anyone looking at his drawing, he folds the drawing in half and hands it in like that. The teacher respects the child's wishes and keeps the paper folded.

Make sure you are careful to keep to this agreement. Be strictly honest in this. Occasionally children will test your reliability and if they find out that you or anyone else did see the drawing, their confidence in you will be damaged.

There comes a moment when a child wants to take a certain drawing home. The child wants to give it as a present to his parents or wants to take it home for some other reason. However, it is better to insist that the drawing remain at school. Chances are pretty high that the parents will not understand what is behind a scratchy drawing that looks like nothing and isn't beautiful. They may make disapproving remarks to the child, and then what?

However, you can use the question of taking the drawing home with them as another opportunity for Focusing: "Is there something in you that really wants to show it at home?" Then you wait to see if something comes.

Children often wonder what will happen to their drawings. Tell them you will hold onto the drawings until the end of the school year. No one will be permitted look at them without the child's approval. At the end of the year the children can review the drawings in their folders. Together you can observe and discuss their development over the course of the school year. At this time you can also discuss what to do with the drawings. Sometimes the teacher keeps them until the children have left school. Then the drawings are destroyed, sometimes in a ritual, with the entire class present.

B. Ending and talking afterwards

You are often restricted by time. That's why you need to be clear about how long the process will last. Give the children a few minutes warning before it's time to stop drawing. Don't be too strict because something may come up during the discussion that urgently needs to be put on paper. So don't clear away the drawing materials until after the group discussion.

"Nothing, no more problems!"

After drawing time, give four or five children the opportunity to talk about their drawings. (Not all children can have a turn; it would take too much time, and attention would flag and boredom set in. The following week, five other children can have a turn.) Ask each of the five if he or she wants to say something. The emphasis is on the word "if." The child is not obliged to say anything. If some child does not want to share, you give that child an opportunity next time. It is an important lesson in the development of self to be able to say "no" and be respected in that decision. It turns out that the willingness to say "yes" often slowly appears.

After five children have spoken, ask if anyone has something really urgent they want to say about their drawing. In this way you don't exclude a child who has worked on something especially difficult.

We have found it best if children don't have to put their hand up to get a turn. Children often put a lot of energy into getting attention, and we have found that this stirs up unnecessary competition. Children often have the feeling that you think they are the nicest, smartest pupil if you choose them, or, on the contrary, the most stupid one if you don't choose them. You can let them learn to trust from the basic Focusing attitude that there is a fair way to divide the turns.

During the discussion afterwards there are a number of items to pay attention to.

> *Koan is a teacher in a primary school. He remembers that he used to ask: "Can you tell me what you have drawn? What is on your paper?"*
>
> *In response the children told him about the content of what they had drawn, but the emotional side of the work was not discussed.*
>
> *Now Koan asks: "What was it like for you to draw this ... does your drawing have something to say to you?"*

Talking about a drawing can evoke emotions. It is not unusual for a child to cry when she speaks about her work. With your empathic attitude you make sure to react with compassion. The other children quickly get used to the fact that children express their emotions. They also learn to react in an empathic and mirroring way. Usually some mirroring from you is sufficient: the sadness is heard. One teacher commented:

> *It was quite a discovery for the children and for me that the toughest boy in the group started to cry. After that we all viewed him differently. He belonged more to the group.*

In the beginning the children often ask: "Do you like my drawing?"
One teacher reported:

> *I myself contributed to these questions, because as a teacher I*
> *am used to praising the children. I used to say of every drawing:*
> *"You did that very well" or "What a beautiful drawing."*
>
> *That contradicts my instructions to them, that the drawing*
> *doesn't have to be beautiful.*
>
> *Because of Focusing I am learning to listen more to what I*
> *say. I notice sooner if I'm not being "with" the child, and then*
> *I change my attitude.*

If you offer children the opportunity, they are capable of understanding
a lot about each other. They quickly learn to accept what the other
says or draws. Another teacher said:

> *Rick is nine years old with a soft voice. He is a quiet, withdrawn*
> *boy who does not stand up for himself very well. During drawing*
> *one day, he explodes and yells: "How do you write 'damn it'?"*
>
> *Cursing is strictly forbidden in our school. While talking about*
> *his drawing he repeats the word in a strong voice. At another*
> *time the children would react disapprovingly to a bad word, but*
> *in this instance it is accepted. The room has gone quiet, because*
> *we understand the importance of that which is changing inside*
> *Rick.*

C. When children do not want or are not allowed to participate

Some parents don't want their child to participate in the program.
You respect this wish.

Sometimes it is the child who does not want to participate.
Again, this preference is respected. You might simply say: "There's
something in you that doesn't want to participate right now."

You can invite the child to draw something, whatever he wants
as long as he doesn't disturb the other children. Usually it isn't long
before this child drifts into participating. You let the child join the
program without any further comment.

D. When nothing comes

For some children, nothing will come when they begin to focus.
Maybe it is too gray, shadowy, or foggy inside. Maybe the child has
simply not yet heard or understood what it feels like there. With
each invitation, let the child check whether something has come
that she can work with.

If not, take some time to be with this child. If there is "nothing," that is OK too. Emphasize that a blank sheet also wants to say something. It has as much to say as a full sheet. Invite the child to pause and be with the emptiness. How does it feel? What does the child notice inside? Does the blank sheet of paper have something to tell?

Sometimes fear impedes a child's drawing, fear that he won't perform well enough, that the drawing won't be good enough. By giving friendly attention to these feelings, a child can let go of the part that feels forced and afraid. In that way he will gain confidence in what he really wants.

E. When children disturb each other

Executing a group program is not always easy. A number of organizational problems must be overcome. Sometimes children disturb each other during Focusing or clearing a space.

> *Wilhelmina is a teacher who has only recently introduced "clearing a space" to her class of six-year-olds.*
>
> *After the exercise, the children show their drawings and talk about them. With each drawing, one student, Rosa, calls out: "Not good at all ... not nice ... very ugly ... " The teacher notices that it is terribly distracting and troubling to the others. Nothing helps to keep Rosa quiet and all of Wilhelmina's attention is on Rosa, while she wants to be with all the children during the discussion. In the end she separates Rosa and seats her to one side.*
>
> *Wilhelmina feels irritated, as if she has failed. She feels badly for having separated Rosa. Thinking about it afterwards, she realizes she can use mirroring: "Something in you feels the need to criticize the drawing ..." It becomes clear to Wilhelmina that "something" could be playing a role in Rosa's behavior. If she can honor this, then Rosa has a little more room for change.*

As teachers learn Focusing, their attitudes change and this helps limit the disturbances. Teachers go from a stance that says, "I, the teacher, know what is good for you and you will do what I want in the way that I want it" to a stance that says: "I trust who you are. Together we will discover what your way may be, with respect for both you and others."

The more experience the children and teachers have with Focusing, the fewer disturbances there will be. There is not only an increase in self-respect but also in respect for other people.

F. When more than one child starts crying at the same time

While clearing a space with your class, it may be that more than one child makes contact with sad feelings at the same time.

> One day during Focusing Miss Maike sees five different children start to cry. She doesn't want to leave any of them alone, but she can't be in five places at once. She asks each crying child to go and sit with a friend. The teacher asks the friends: "Can you listen to him or her in a kind way?"
>
> Miss Maike has already taught the children how to mirror each other. She notices now how valuable it is. Mirroring skills enable the children in her class to help each other and to support her efforts as well.

In this example, clearing a space was combined with listening in a mirroring way. Because of the skills of other children, the sadness of all five children was heard. That is a very different way of dealing with each other than eternal criticism or backbiting. Even more children will be heard and supported when children integrate Focusing into their everyday interactions with each other.

6

Specific Applications

Once children are familiar with Focusing, it can be integrated into their lives in a variety of ways. There are micro-processes or short Focusing exercises that you can use very quickly, as well as longer workshops. Some of these require very little of your time; others require several sessions. Some do not require the child to know Focusing, others require some familiarity.

MICRO-PROCESSES

Children especially are quick to change their feelings, sometimes with just a few Focusing steps. This is true even for physical pain. For instance, once sensory awareness had been taught (Step A in Chapter 4, *Teaching Focusing to Groups,* p. 45), Marc (age 11) had more awareness of his body, and his teacher could easily refer to it to help him.

> *Marc's arm, shoulder and fingers all hurt when he is holding his*
> *pencil. His teacher, in a quick, individual interaction, says:*
> *Teacher*: How does it feel in your shoulder?
> *Marc*: It's like iron ... and now it becomes softer!

Reflection:
> *It takes very little time to complete a micro-process, and, in*
> *this case, a basic introduction to Focusing is all it took to lead*
> *one.*

Marc's awareness of his body enabled him to let go of his tension. A girl in another class looked at her teacher with a very confused expression when the teacher asked if she was aware that she was permanently pulling her shoulders up high. Unlike Marc, she had never attended a class in which sensory awareness or clearing a space had been taught.

But even if the child hasn't had Focusing training, the teacher can use his or her own knowledge of Focusing to help. For example, in another situation, six-year-old Mieke had a splinter in her thumb.

During recess she approached her teacher.

Mieke: Ouch, I have a splinter here, and it hurts.

Teacher: A sore thumb because of a splinter. Did this just happen in the playground?

Mieke: No, I got it at home.

Teacher: You got it at home ... and how should that splinter move out of your finger?

Mieke: Well, my mom was supposed to do it.

Teacher: Mom was supposed to do that.

Mieke: Ouch, ouch, it hurts again right now.

Teacher: When you press on it, you feel it.

Mieke: Yes, but not now.

Teacher: If you press on it a little differently then it doesn't.

Mieke: Ouch, ouch, now it hurts again.

Teacher: Inside you know exactly how to make it hurt and how to leave it alone ... I have a needle here we could use to pick it out.

Mieke: Does it hurt?

Teacher: Yes ... the needle makes a little prick. Prick! Then the splinter is out and it won't bother you anymore.

Mieke: But does it hurt a lot?

Teacher: Not very much. Maybe we can prick it out.

Mieke: Yes, but I don't want it to hurt very much.

Teacher: No, you don't want it to hurt very much. We will take a good look at it. Like this ... a good look at it in the light. Shall we say something nice to the little splinter?

Mieke: Hello, hello.

Teacher: Yes, and then...

Mieke: How are you doing? Ouch, ouch.

Teacher: Shall we ask what it needs?

Mieke: Yes.

Teacher: Go ahead and ask ... What do you need? What does this little splinter say?

Mieke: I need a prick, ... ouch, ouch.

Teacher: I need a prick because then ...

Mieke: Because if we have a little prick, ouch, ouch ...

Teacher: If we make a small opening, right?

Mieke: Ouch, ouch ...

Teacher: The splinter knows that it needs the little needle to prick it out.

Mieke: Yes.

Teacher: Yes, the splinter says yes to the little needle.

Mieke: Ouch.

Teacher: You can also pinch my arm with your other hand. OK? Does that help a little?

Mieke: Ouch, OUCH.

Teacher: Yes, it really hurts.

Mieke: No.

Teacher: It is quite hard, isn't it?

Mieke: OUCH ... I want you to stop it.

Teacher: You want me to stop it ... well, look here, it is already on the needle ... you wanted me to stop when the little splinter was already out ...

Mieke: No.

Teacher: Just look here ... Shall we say: thanks, thumb for being so brave?

Mieke: Thank you, thumb.

Reflection:

• *While this is not a Focusing process per se, you can see here the teacher's basic Focusing attitude, especially in the words she uses. This attitude gives Mieke the space she needs to conquer her fear of pain.*

• *Focusing language is often used to talk to the body or a part of the body. If someone is friendly with what is there, it can bring about a different relationship to uncomfortable physical sensations, like pain.*

In a similar micro-process, teachers use the basic Focusing attitude for brief emotional interactions. In this way difficulties clear up quickly. When a child is angry, teachers not only ask about the cause, they also make a connection with the child's felt sense, as in: "You are very angry. Where do you notice the anger in your body? How does it feel there?" With reflection of this kind, the children take more responsibility for their behavior and feelings. When they are in touch with their felt sense, they don't have to point to someone else with all kinds of accusations.

In some schools, teachers have individual sessions with children when there are problems.

Seven-year-old Martin's face turns white whenever he hears that the class will be going to the swimming pool. Earlier in the day, the teacher tried to persuade him to go by saying:

"Oh, you silly boy ... I know that you can do it ... the others do it ... I will look after you ... you can't drown ...!"

Now the teacher says something different: "Something inside you is afraid, isn't it? Where is it? And what is happening

inside at this moment? ... Can you be nice to it?"
Martin's face brightens.

Reflection:

- *It doesn't take a lot of time. If Martin directs his attention to the fear inside, there is change. The point at first is not to overcome the fear, but to listen to the part of himself which is frightened. This can only be done if the teacher is with Martin for a moment, supporting him.*
- *Sometimes the teacher gives Martin a sheet of paper so he can draw his fear, an hour before the group goes swimming. Recently Martin has been making progress with his swimming lessons.*

AFFIRMING BOUNDARIES

Focusing can help teachers set boundaries in a clear and respectful way. Sometimes adults find themselves forbidding children's behaviors left and right until every interaction devolves into a contest of wills. Use of the basic Focusing attitude can prevent this from happening.

Even when a child's behavior needs to be stopped, it is important to acknowledge the wish underlying it. "You want to throw that clay so much ... but that is not possible here." You do not accept the behavior, but you acknowledge the child's wants and feelings. This is crucial, because the child's wish is closely connected to his sense of self. Often, a child is prepared to adjust his actions if he feels heard and received in this way.

If you maintain the rules while communicating respect for the child, you can help that child grow. Indeed, the moments when boundaries are challenged are often excellent growing opportunities for children.

At a day care center, the oldest children, the three-year-olds, are not permitted to run because it disturbs the babies sleeping on the floor below. The teachers are constantly reminding the children to stop running. They repeat this over and over throughout the day. By the end of the day the teachers are often irritated and reprimand the children: "Why can't you ever listen? This running is bad behavior!" The teachers report that they find themselves saying these things even though they hate doing so.

Mirroring is a way for them to change their response and alter their irritation around running. Now they simply say: "You are running. Your little feet are running across the floor. You love running so much but you can't do it here." The children stop right away as if they are thinking, "Oh yes, that's true."

Reflection:

• *Can you imagine how relieved the teachers must have been when they discovered mirroring? Now it is the children who decide to stop running; the directive is no longer imposed from the outside. It's as though the children are saying with their bodies, "It's a good thing you're reminding me of this."*
• *Of course, children are forgetful and often do not sustain a new behavior for long. After a few minutes, they may start running again. But by offering a mirroring response instead of a reprimanding response, the teachers are able to draw a clear boundary and at the same time convey their respect for the children's independence and self-worth.*

Story

In Germany, Bettina uses Focusing with her class of eleven-year-olds at a school for children with special needs. One day, Bettina leads a project about Native Americans. At the end of class, she and the three girls in her small group roast popcorn and eat it.

Three of the boys in the class take part in a different project about Europe. When they return and see the girls eating popcorn, they fly off the handle. They say they were having a terrible time in their group and they want to eat popcorn too. Unfortunately, there is no more oil for making popcorn. Bettina proposes instead to roast popcorn for the whole class the following day. This does not appease the boys.

Two of them want to speak to Bettina privately. They tell her how boring their group project was and how unfair they think it is that the other group got to have popcorn. Bettina mirrors all of this, but the boys remain very angry. She asks what they would like to see happen. They say they want to make popcorn the next day and they want to be the only ones who get to eat it. Bettina mirrors this and then explains that she cannot accept their condition. She says once more that she is happy to make popcorn for the whole class. The boys turn away, angry and defensive. Bettina reflects their body language in words. She expresses what she thinks their thoughts and feelings might be. None of this brings a response.

Bettina faces a dilemma. She wants to support the boys, but she notices that it is very important for her not to give up on her condition that popcorn be made for the whole class. She tells the boys how it is for her. She repeats her offer and then returns to the class. She tells the other children that no solution has yet been reached. Then, the third boy proposes to speak to his friends. After just thirty seconds he returns to the class, beaming, and asks Bettina to join him in the other room. She finds the other two boys smiling. As soon as they see her they shout in unison: "Tomorrow we want to make popcorn with everyone or else we'll never come back to this stupid school!" Bettina laughs along with the boys.

The next day the whole class makes popcorn together and eats it while they talk about their projects. There is a sense of harmony in the room. Even when Bettina gives out a writing assignment, the children do not protest.

Reflection:

• *Notice the power of mirroring in this example. The mirroring does not produce a solution, but it does keep the anger from escalating.*

• *Bettina sets a clear boundary and maintains it. She repeats her stance in a neutral, non-accusatory way that makes her own position clear, while leaving the boys' sense of worth intact.*

• *Ultimately, the boys are empowered to make their own choice within the boundaries established by their teacher. She does not force anything on them.*

"LONELY ... BULLYING ...
Bang Crack Boom"

AGGRESSION AND BULLYING

Occasionally children do get into fights with each other. Afterwards adults are often inclined to decide which child is to blame. They want to side with the victim. We can forget that the feelings of the aggressor also need care and attention. Focusing allows us to communicate respect for both children's inner worlds without excusing behavior that is against the rules. We can mirror the inner needs and feelings of both.

Another way to prepare children to see both sides of an argument is to hold a workshop on bullying similar to this one in Budapest.

Klara, an experienced focuser, teaches at a middle school. For a few months she has used Focusing with her class, guiding them toward a felt sense and showing them how to mirror each other.

Recently Klara's school has experienced several incidents of bullying. Klara wants to give her students the chance to explore their feelings around bullying and being bullied. She also wants to help them figure out what to do if they witness a fight.

Preparation:
Klara brings her class to the school's spacious library and divides them into groups of three. Each group receives three brightly colored medals that they can hang around their necks. The medals say "the bullier," "the bullied," and "the helper."

Introduction:
Klara helps the children focus their attention. She invites them to notice their breathing and the feeling of their legs and backs against the chairs. She leads a short discussion, asking questions such as: "Who bullies sometimes?" "Who has a problem with bullying?" "How do you react when someone else is being bullied?"

Explanation:
Klara explains that the medals indicate which role each child is playing. The role of the bully is to insult and harass. The role of the bullied is to respond. The role of the helper is to mirror the words and actions of both. After five minutes of this, the children will stop and discuss what they experienced with their partners. Then they will switch roles. They will do this three times so that every child has the chance to experience all three roles. Klara tells them that no touching will be allowed during the game.

Exercise:
As the groups do the exercise, Klara moves between them, observing and offering support where it is needed. After all three rounds are completed, she distributes the children's Focusing notebooks. She helps the children bring their attention inside, saying, "Ask yourself what it is like to be the bullied child. Where do you feel that inside? What does it feel like? What comes from there? Can you express that on paper? What color would be just right for it? Don't worry about making it

pretty—your hand knows just how it should be drawn. Now flip to the next page. Ask inside: What does it feel like to be the bully? Where in you do you feel that?"

Klara gives the children time to focus on each of the three roles. At the end, she asks them whether their drawings have something to say. Several children report that they were surprised to discover that as the bully they felt afraid.

Reflection:

In order to engage in such an activity, children must be familiar with Focusing and mirroring. Once they are, they can have real insight not only into their own experiences, but into the experiences of others.

A SOCIAL SKILLS WORKSHOP

Erik Verliefde, from the Netherlands, has been leading counseling groups for young teens for many years. He has in fact written a book called *Growing Pains in Social Contact* (see *Appendix*, p. 159) He incorporates Focusing into teaching social skills and assertiveness training. He prepares by connecting first to his own Focusing attitude. That way when disruptions arise or strong emotions are expressed, he can respond in a Focusing way. During the workshop, he leads participants in five Focusing exercises: writing their names expressively, finding a safe place inside, making contact with what's inside, clearing a space, and listening to each other in a mirroring way.

In the first meeting, Erik passes out notebooks and invites participants to write their names expressively, in a way that conveys something about who they are and how they want to be seen. (See Step B in Chapter 7, *Focusing Variations*, p.74.) Some young people write their names very simply. Others draw an elaborate picture with their name as part of it. The participants then write their names in each other's notebooks.

Next, Erik leads the group members in finding a safe place within their bodies. Using a model established by Jooske Kool, he leads them on a search for a friend or an ally inside. He uses fantasy to encourage the finding of this "inner friend." Once the friend has been found, the youngster and the friend go in search of a safe place. Erik guides the process using the following text:

Your inner friend asks you to come to a special place, where it is warm and safe ... You follow him, he is taking you there ... Take a good look at what this place looks

*like, notice how it feels, how it smells and what you
hear ... Go and sit down with your inner friend. Get
comfortable. Maybe your inner friend has something to
tell you, something about you ... Or maybe there is a
question you would like to ask your inner friend ... a
question about something that is bothering you,
something that's been on your mind ...*

From this safe place the participants make contact made with what's
inside. Erik does not teach Focusing explicitly, but he uses important
parts of the process.

Often at the start of a session, Erik leads the group in clearing a
space. Sometimes he plans to do this. Other times the students
request it. The young people arrive filled with thoughts and feelings,
everything from not wanting to be there because they'd rather be at
a drawing class to being intensely excited about picking up a puppy
to take home later that day. Erik uses the image of a bucket as a
container for everything the participants find when they clear a space.
He says to them:

*Visualize a bucket. Put everything that's bothering you in that
bucket. Your fears, your anger, your sadness, your worries,
your irritation ... all the bad things that have happened ... put it
all in the bucket. Imagine that a big yellow hot air balloon is
attached to the bucket. Now watch as that bucket filled with
all the bad things is lifted off the ground and rises into the air.
It goes higher and higher, getting smaller and smaller until it
disappears completely. Now take a deep breath and notice all
the space there is inside you ...*

Erik teaches the members of his social skills group how to ask for
what they need, how to digest criticism, and how to draw boundaries.
Partway into the workshop, he teaches them an important Focusing
partnership skill: listening in a mirroring way. All along Erik has modeled
mirroring. When it comes time for the group to learn, they are already
somewhat familiar with the technique.

Erik finds that Focusing makes a valuable contribution to his
workshops. The participants' enthusiasm for the process is apparent
by the way they spontaneously ask to clear a space or, without
prompting, begin to mirror when someone is telling a story. All these
Focusing techniques support the development of problem solving,
social cognition, and behavioral skills.

7

Focusing Variations

It can be fun to add some variety to the Focusing process. The exercises in this section suggest a variety of themes and structures for your Focusing sessions with children.

A. Clearing a space on the map of your body

Invite a child or group of children to clear a space in a special way. Ask them to draw their bodies on large sheets of paper. You can even have them lie down while other children outline their bodies. Next, invite them to color their body image and to write or make pictures of the things they feel inside. You can prompt them in various ways:

> What do you notice that feels good in your life? Where in your
>   body do you notice that? Can you give a color to it? Draw it
>   just the way your hand wants it to be drawn.
> What is difficult in your life? What is preventing you from feeling
>   happy and relaxed? What colors go with that feeling? How
>   does all of this want to be drawn on the picture of your
>   body?

B. Writing and saying your name

As long as children know how to write, they can participate in this exercise. You ask them to represent their names as expressively as they feel them inside. The goal is for children to explore their identities and affirm the power of their names. Invite the children as follows:

> Check inside to see whether your sheet of paper wants to be
>   lying sideways or upright or on a diagonal ... Where on the
>   paper does your name want to be drawn? ... How large or
>   how small does it want to be? What kind of letters would be
>   just right? What kind of colors come with those letters?
>   Take a quiet moment to check inside ... How does your
>   name want to be decorated? Really take time to sense it.
>   How does your hand want to move? As you draw, stop and

check if the drawing fits with the feeling inside. Is it finished? Is there something else that belongs on the page? Wait for the moment when you sense inside that it is just right.

You can finish by asking:

Who wants to talk about what that was like?
Does your drawing have something else it wants to say?

You can also ask children to explore how their names want to be said out loud. Allow the children to sense inside and then, one by one, pronounce their names in a special "just right" way. Invite the group to repeat the name, mirroring the child's volume and inflection. Some children like to have their names said very quietly. Others like to hear their names sung. Some children will evoke the voices of parents, grandparents, teachers, or special moments in their lives.

One boy discovered that he liked to hear his name as though it were being said by a voice far away. He realized that this was a memory of when he came out of general anesthesia a year earlier. When the boys in the group repeated his name in this way, he recalled the experience of waking up.

This is a wonderful activity for children who are getting to know each other. It can also be an enjoyable activity for a birthday party.

C. Making self-portraits

Making self-portraits allows children to consider both how they are seen and how they experience themselves. Remind the children that their self-portraits do not have to be beautiful. You can reassure them by making your own self-portrait. (Make your portrait less

skillful and complete than theirs because you don't want them to be discouraged when they look at your drawing.) If you have clay available, you can also try this exercise three-dimensionally. With small children, start with a flat two-dimensional block of clay.

Whatever medium is used, when the self-portrait is finished, ask each child: "What does this face have to say to you?" Children may discover something unexpected about themselves or share something important about their self-image.

D. Hanging worries on a tree

When they clear a space, children are to imagine some place where they can leave their worries safely. It is usually helpful for them to make this safe space concrete. One way to do this is by constructing a big paper tree and pasting it to the wall of the children's classroom. As they clear a space, ask the children to write or draw each worry on a colored piece of paper and paste it to the tree: Have them leave the piece of paper open if they want others to see the worry or folded if the worry is private. The tree can be used just once or it can become a permanent feature of the room and a consistent tool for clearing a space.

E. The bear's dream

Agnes, a kindergarten teacher in Budapest, uses this activity to help children connect to a felt sense. She and her class sit down on the floor. Agnes and her assistant play the mother bears while all the children play the bear cubs. The cubs close their eyes. The mother bears sing a lullaby to help the bear cubs turn their attention inside. Agnes says: "Let yourself have a dream. There's something inside that wants to be heard. Do you notice a feeling? Give some attention to it." Afterwards, the children share. Often their "dreams" are everyday experiences, but the feelings are shared in a meaningful way.

F. The lion's game

The lion's game helps children connect to angry and aggressive feelings inside. Guide the children in turning their attention inward. Ask them to imagine that they are lions. Ask them to consider what quality they need most from a lion. As they are drawn into the experience, ask them to notice what it feels like inside their bodies. Ask the children to walk around the room like lions, then to walk up to each other as though they were lions. Let them know that these lions are not allowed to touch each other. Then ask them to sit down and draw what it felt like. You can end by asking a few questions such as, "What does your drawing have to say?" "What was that experience like?" Note that other frightening creatures can be substituted for lions, depending on the age and interests of the children.

G. Starting from a story

Sometimes, you can evoke a child's inner story by reading a book out loud. As you read, encourage the child to let his or her attention go inside. Invite them to choose a character or an event from the story. With your questions, help them link the story to their own inner experience.

> *What was the most important part of the story for you? What was the scariest part? What was the happiest part? Notice what that feels like in your body. You can color that feeling, or draw a picture of it or write about it ... Whatever comes is just fine ... even if it's a blank sheet of paper.*

In this way, you help the child make a connection from the feelings in the story to his own experiences.

H. Elevator ride

Lucy, a teacher and Focusing trainer in Canada, has developed this Focusing technique for children between the ages of six and ten. She invites them to step inside an elevator and take a trip down into themselves. After preparing the children, by having them imagine what an elevator looks like and creating an imaginary one in their mind's eye, she talks about how, among the many buttons to push, there is one that is labeled "Story."

> *Imagine you are inside your elevator... there are buttons you can push to have a little visit to different parts of you to see how they are feeling today. Perhaps we could start by going down to your toes and saying hello to them. They may like it if you step out of the elevator and have a real visit ... [Visit various parts of the body]*
> *Remember your special "story" button? This is a very important button because when it is pushed, the elevator gets to go wherever it wants to go. The elevator will take you to a place inside your body that holds a story and you may not yet know where that is or what that is about ...*

Please remember that you have a stop button in case you feel the need to stop along the way. Also remember you are in charge of your elevator. Whenever you are ready to push that special button, please do so ... [Give them plenty of time]

Notice where the elevator takes you now. Perhaps you want to stay in the elevator and observe your story from in there. Maybe you could open the door. How does it look? How does it feel? Do you wish to step out and explore your story? Who else is there? What is happening? [Allow some time and observe the group closely. It is not unusual to see some squirming, distractions or even tears. Let them know, if they come to a tough spot, to be gentle with that part of the story.]

Boys and girls, I am going to ask you to find a way to say goodbye to your story and let it know that you will come back to it another time. Please notice how it feels when you go back into the elevator ... push the button to close the door ... find the button you need to come back ... When everyone has their eyes open we will move quietly to our desks and begin writing or sharing something about our stories.

The power of the trip inside the elevator lies in the special way the child lets her attention go inside. It is also very important to emphasize that the child controls the buttons. That means she gets to decide where and how the elevator goes.

FOCUSING ABOUT SPECIAL TOPICS

Once children are familiar with Focusing, you can then give them specific topics to focus about. You might say to them:
Notice what happens inside when ...
- *you're going to a birthday party*
- *you think about the night*
- *you're with a friend*
- *you don't have a friend*
- *you go to school*
- *you're on vacation*
- *you're sick*

Sometimes you can introduce subjects that are relevant to the whole class, such as preparing for a special lesson or a school trip. Often your students will offer ideas about what to focus on: an event that has affected their class, their country, or the entire world. Remember that the heart of Focusing is engaging the felt sense. Be sure to help the children connect what they say to what they feel inside.

You can also set up a role-play around a particular theme. Afterwards, the children can use Focusing to connect to what it felt like to play each role. Or you may ask, "What is the most important thing you learned from this experience?"

PREPARING FOR TESTS

Even when children are well prepared to take a test, their nervousness can interfere with their performance. It turns out that young people perform better when they have taken time to connect to their bodies, preparing the inner environment for the stress it is about to experience. Clearing a space is an excellent way to do this.

It is also helpful for children to focus on the tension from its point of view, to discover what the nervousness itself is feeling. By making contact with the feeling in a friendly, open way, they can understand it, reduce its charge, and come to discover the meaning behind it.

Drawing and coloring helps children put all of this on paper so that it is concrete and they can regard it from a distance. This symbolizing process dramatically eases the tension inside, and leaves a lot more room for the child to cope with the pressure of the test itself.

If the teacher agrees, it can be productive for the child to scribble down some notes about what she is feeling even as she is taking the test. Simply making contact with the feeling and then putting it aside can make an enormous difference.

"SUCCEED!"

GOING TO THE HOSPITAL

The comments in this section can be applied to a range of medical interventions, including routine activities such as check-ups and vaccinations, in fact, wherever parents and primary caregivers are closely involved in preparing children for the event and processing the experience afterwards. Teachers and medical professionals will find in this section a child-centered approach to treatment and recovery.

For almost all children, the prospect of being hospitalized is threatening: at best it is a source of tension; at worst it is downright terrifying. Focusing can help a child prepare for this unfamiliar experience in a couple of important ways. By engaging the felt sense, the child contacts a deeper layer of feeling than the one accessed in normal conversation. This lays the groundwork for him to maintain a sense of control and inner strength in the face of intrusive procedures.

A child-care provider's own experience with hospitalization will influence how he or she relates to the event. It is therefore invaluable for adults to focus first on their own feelings. Doing so creates more space for the child and a greater openness to how the child feels about the experience.

No matter how young the child is, honesty is truly the best policy. It is the basis for her trust in you. Give the child all the information that you have in a manner that is age-appropriate and respectful of her fantasies. For example, you might ask, "How do you think it will go? What do you imagine it will be like?"

Next, give some attention to the child's felt sense. The tried-and-true Focusing-oriented questions will serve you well here: "Where in your body do you feel all that? How does it feel there? As you sit with it, does an image or a color appear? Do you want to draw that?" Symbolizing from the felt sense can ease — and ultimately transform—fear and insecurity.

It is also helpful for a child to track his felt sense as he imagines, step by step, everything that will take place in the hospital. This allows his inner self to prepare for the experience. Start by helping the child find a safe space inside and/or safe colors to work with. It will be important for you to bring a lot of empathy to this exercise, as well as some creative thinking as you hypothesize about what the child might be feeling. This is especially the case with a very young child who cannot easily put his feelings into words.

Here are some of the questions you can ask:

Can you imagine yourself walking through the doors of the hospital?

Can you imagine lying in your bed at the hospital?

Can you imagine the nurse coming to give you a shot?

Can you see a needle coming toward you? Can you say "yes" to it?

What would your finger or your arm or your leg need in order to allow that needle to push into it?

Can you imagine going into a deep sleep so that the doctor can operate?

What does it need inside to allow that sleep to come?

> *What does it need inside to trust the doctor's hands as she operates?*
>
> *Can you be nice to the pain that might be there when you wake up, even though you don't want it?*

You may want to provide some words of reassurance as well:

> *We are not going to be there with you, but we will be thinking of you the whole time. When it's over we'll come back again.*
>
> *When you feel lonely you can wrap your arms around that lonely feeling and be nice to it like a friend.*

Often, loneliness is one of the most upsetting parts of a child's time in the hospital. If, in your preparatory Focusing, you can help him connect to his felt sense, it will bolster his confidence in his ability to handle the experience. This confidence-building process may not happen in words. Be sure to bring along some paper and crayons so that the child has the chance to symbolize what he feels inside.

FOCUSING WITH DREAMS AND NIGHTMARES

Listening to a nightmare and the story it tells can actually ease the fear of it. And when the message of a dream has been worked through, the dream typically does not recur.

Eugene Gendlin teaches that every dream offers the possibility of a forward motion. You can help a child get at the meaning of a dream through symbolizing it on paper. As the child's Focusing companion you can ask, "How would you like the dream to proceed? How would you like it to end?"

"Nightmare"

Roy is ten years old. He is an anxious child who often has difficulty concentrating. One day, while clearing a space, he exhibits strong feelings but is unable to express himself to the group. It seems to his teacher that he is especially withdrawn for the rest of the day. After school, Roy's teacher makes time for him. Roy explains that he has been having scary dreams in which a ghost appears. He says that he is ready to draw the ghost. When Roy's drawing is complete, his teacher asks if the picture has anything it wants to say. Roy

turns to the ghost and says: "Go away."

Roy draws the ghost again a few days later and then it disappears altogether from his dreams. In the following weeks, he seems a bit more confident than before.

Another example:

Jaap attends a special school for the mentally challenged. In class he sits motionless. He appears to be very disconnected from his body. Jaap tells Marta about a frequently recurring dream.

Jaap: There is a wall and there are traffic lights and I can't get through ... that's all I know.

Marta: A wall and traffic lights ... You can't get through ... How is that in your body?

Jaap: A hard feeling and also empty ...

Marta: Hard and empty ... Could you draw or paint all that?

Jaap: (nodding) Yes ... paint ...

He paints a large red field, a black traffic signal with three lights, one of which he paints red. Then he paints a thick black line representing the wall.

Jaap: I can't get through ... I can't get out ...

Marta: Does anything happen inside when you can't get out?

Jaap: Yes, it gets very quiet ... as if there's nothing anymore ...

Marta: Quiet ... as if nothing is there anymore ...

Jaap draws a ladder against the wall.

Marta: A ladder comes ...

Jaap: I climb over the wall and now I am going to do something else ...

Suddenly, Jaap gets up to go. It is the first time he has ever done such a thing spontaneously.

Reflection:

• *Focusing is a self-guided process. In this story Marta did not have to think up clever questions or offer an interpretation. Her only task was to connect to the basic Focusing attitude and be present with the Focuser.*

• *As a companion you need never worry that the Focuser is going in the wrong direction. You simply trust the inner process. The Focuser knows the right way to go.*

8

Listening and Mirroring

A teacher is wondering: "I organize a group discussion in my third grade class every day. Because I have a small class everyone can have a turn. The children are approximately eight years old. It takes a little while before these eight-year-olds learn not to interrupt each other, and to allow others to have their say. However, it's extremely difficult to have children actually listen to each other. You have the impression that when one child has told her story, then she feels she's done! How can I get children to really listen to each other during group discussion?"

A mother asks: "My son is in his third year of high school. I never succeed in discussing anything with him. Each time that I want to negotiate he silences me: "Mom, you're impossible to talk with." I try to listen, but each time he keeps saying that I don't like him, that he has a mother who only complains. How can I talk to my son?"

There is a lot of literature about listening to children, (e.g. *Teacher Effectiveness Training* by Tom Gordon; *Emotional Intelligence* by Daniel Goleman and *How to Talk so Kids Will Listen and Listen So Kids Will Talk* by Faber & Mazlish, see Bibliography). They all conclude that listening is a powerful, but not well understood technique. Listening is not just asking thoughtful questions, nor quietly nodding and saying little. What good listening means here is a special kind of paying attention that enables a child to feel heard, and even more, understood.

Many people do not know that simply by giving non-judgmental attention, you can facilitate a child's development. It is amazing but true; when you really listen to a young person, it releases in them a space for their own direction, and for solutions that are often surprising and constructive. You want to learn this special type of listening because it creates change.

Focusing teaches this type of listening. It also offers a teachable description of what needs to happen *inside the speaker, as well as the listener,* in order for change to take place. For instance, both you and the child pay attention to *inner feelings.* You both understand how to be with a *felt sense.*

KEYS TO GOOD LISTENING

There are various steps to good listening. You will need to learn:
- to practice a number of sub-steps
- to observe the other person carefully
- to notice non-verbal messages
- to cultivate an attitude of acceptance, at least of the speaker's emotions and feelings, if not his behavior
- to eliminate language on your part that blocks communication
- to reflect back what is being communicated, even as a mirror reflects an image

Sub-steps
Listening as a basic skill seems so self-evident that we don't realize it is really a combination of sub-steps. Goleman in his book *Emotional Intelligence* has split up listening into five small steps, each of equal value.

Posture. By assuming a certain posture, you make it visually clear that you are listening. You direct your body towards the speaker, you turn your head towards the speaker, and you are not fiddling with something.

Looking at the other person. Making eye contact is essential. You don't want to stare at the other person while listening, but making eye contact every now and again encourages the process.

Giving short reactions. Nodding now and again indicates that you are attentive. This non-verbal behavior encourages the speaker to continue. There are various verbal reactions that have this same effect: "uh-huh," "hmm," "really?"

Asking for more information. There may be things the speaker mentions that you do not understand or subjects that you'd like to know more about: "What did she say?" or "I don't understand that!" or "With how many children?" This asking for information does not imply any judgment, commentary, or advice. The child is stimulated to give a clearer picture of the situation and as a result the picture becomes clearer for the child too.

Saying what you think of it. During listening it is better not to say what you think. You don't want to interrupt the other person or impose your meaning on the subject. After the speaker finishes, however, it is appropriate to give just one sentence that lets them know what you've taken away from their story: "That sounds like a nice experience," or "It's too bad things happened that way," or "Wow, what a story!"

Focusing listening involves these same components, although you do not usually ask for concrete information. In Focusing, the speaker does not have to reveal any details about the situation she is dealing with, although she can if she likes. More likely we ask her, "How does all that feel inside?"

Observing
Your ability to observe affects your listening skill. During communication with children you observe attentively, without drawing conclusions or interpreting what you hear. Children (or adults, for that matter) know best what is going on inside themselves. They are the authorities on their own experiences. What children say may sometimes be confusing or incomprehensible to an adult, but by observing closely, and without necessarily giving in immediately to what they want, you will see that children often work out a solution by themselves.

> *A ten-year-old girl is sitting on the floor of the school hallway. She is hugging her knees and scowling. A teacher approaches. The teacher does not know the child's name or what class she is in. The first thing the teacher does is stop, stand there, and look at her with an open face.*
>
> *Then the teacher tries to give words to what she is seeing, without judgment, disapproval or interpretation. Her response is very bare, without frills.*

Teacher: There you are …
The girl looks annoyed
Teacher: All alone …
The girl mutters something unintelligible
Teacher: … and grumbling a little.
The girl nods quickly, still angry
Teacher: It seems like you're sitting there feeling a little angry.
Girl: I am.
Teacher: A little angry.
Girl: Yes because the sun is shining.
Teacher: *(surprised)* The sun is shining and that makes you

angry inside.

Girl: I want to play in the snow.

Teacher: You want to play in the snow. And now you're sitting here in the hallway and you are angry.

Girl: When the sun is shining, the snow melts and I don't want that.

Teacher: You love to play in the snow and when the sun in shining, the snow disappears and then you are angry ... Where is that feeling of anger inside?

Girl: In my tummy.

Teacher: Something in your tummy is angry and you are here stuck with it.

Girl: *(Her face opens up)* Oh well, it's not that bad.

She stands up and disappears in the direction of her class, skipping.

Reflection:

Do you notice how the teacher follows the girl throughout this interaction? She makes up nothing additional, offers no commentary, other than the question, "Where do you feel that inside?" That is the reason why the girl's mood can change and she can let go of her resentful attitude. She does it herself. The girl gets the feeling that she is the master of her own actions and behavior. When you listen in this way, you give children the space to take their own experience seriously, and you enable them, with no pressure, to change and grow in their own way.

Noticing non-verbal messages

When we communicate, we convey more than just our words. How and when we say things carries information that a listener picks up. This is why communication breaks down when listening is not authentic, that is, when we give the impression of listening without really doing it. If, as soon as there is a pause in the conversation, the teacher says in effect, "Now let's stop talking and you go ahead and do what I told you earlier," this communication gives the impression that he or she hasn't been listening. The teacher doesn't want to hear about what his student wants; he just needs her to follow his instructions.

On the other hand, if the teacher were to abandon his authority and say, in effect, "Oh, just go and do whatever you want," this reaction seems to indicate that he doesn't care. He is giving in because he doesn't want to be disturbed. However, if a teacher continues to listen well to the student, it may seem to take more time initially, but because of it, future problems are alleviated, problems that would take more time to solve. The child doesn't have to spend time and energy resisting his teacher's demands. He can and frequently does find a solution that satisfies them both.

Accepting feelings, not behavior

What would it be like if, during communication, you took up a position *with* a child, rather than "for" or "against" them? Being *with a child* means accepting them the way they are and giving them kindly attention. It is a nice, neutral attitude that is firm and clear, with respect for the uniqueness of the child.

If you accept children the way they are, you accept and trust their desires and wishes. However, this does not mean that you permit negative behavior. You accept what is behind a child's negative behavior, such as anger. This does not mean that you allow the child to throw crayons. You say what you see: "You are angry that you are not allowed to color now." At the same time you put a stop to unacceptable actions: "That does not mean that you can throw things."

So while you might "admonish and give orders" concerning a child's behavior, you "allow and accept" his or her emotions and intentions.

Avoiding language that blocks acceptance

Our language contains many words and expressions that prevent acceptance and trust, words that evaluate or judge a child's remarks. Admonishing and moralizing, warnings, orders and criticism, if applied to the child's feelings, can make the child stop talking, as a result of which the communication ends. By using such language, the inner process ceases to develop, and sometimes provocative, rebellious behavior is stirred up. There is some language therefore that we want to avoid in Focusing.

Gordon in his *Effectiveness Training* lists a number of categories to avoid when practicing what he calls "active listening":
- swearing, ridiculing, shaming
- ordering, controlling, commanding
- warning, reprimanding, threatening
- admonishing, moralizing, preaching
- advising, offering solutions yourself
- lecturing, talking pedantically, bringing in logical arguments, judging, criticizing, disagreeing, accusing
- questioning, interrogating, asking questions, interpreting, analyzing, diagnosing
- praising, agreeing, giving compliments
- reassuring, empathizing, comforting, supporting
- withdrawing, distracting, giving in, talking about something else

Everyone agrees that certain adult reactions inhibit development, such as ridiculing and shaming a child in the eyes of friends. It is more difficult to realize that praising or giving a compliment can also impede a child's growth by circumventing how a child might feel about the event. In the everyday life of a child, some praise and complimenting contribute to a healthy sense of self-esteem. However, if the child starts performing only on the basis of expecting and needing adult approval, the sense of his own wishes gets clouded.

> *Two grandparents are on the beach with their grandchildren. The children find the foundation of an old restaurant. They walk along the ledges, balancing themselves, and then jump off into the sand as far as possible. Enthusiastic, the grandmother, calls out: "Hey, you are jumping really far!" Grandparents love to give compliments. They want so much for their grandchildren to feel good. The grandmother hopes that her compliments will encourage her granddaughters to jump further and further. When the younger granddaughter jumps a little bit further, grandmother calls out: "See, you have already jumped further than before."*
>
> *The girl visibly tries hard to jump further. But is she is doing it only for her grandmother? Is the motivation coming from within or without? A little later the girl sees that she cannot improve on her performance. With her head hung down and a sad face, she sighs: "I can't jump far at all." Her disappointment appears greater than her pleasure.*

Reflection:
> • *You may believe in the value of rewards such as praising and giving compliments. However, the effect is not always positive. A compliment can stimulate but it can also curb the child's inner motivation.*
> • *How would it sound to you if grandmother had said: "You really like jumping off that ledge, don't you?"*

MIRRORING

Listening in a mirroring mode takes active listening a step further. When you listen in this mode you reflect back to the child, with your words and gestures, what you observe. The child sees herself as if in a mirror, she hears herself via you. She also experiences your reflective words and gestures as efforts by you to accept and understand her.

Listening in this way is an active process where you must pay close attention in order to play your role. By reflecting thoughts and feelings, you enable children to pay close attention to themselves. You slow down their own reflections, which help them better understand what they are communicating. The effect of the mirroring mode is that the child has time to think about his own words.

Experience and study show that mirroring alone can bring about change, since mirroring implies no judgment or disapproval, yet does encourage the problem-solving capabilities of the child.

> *The Greyston Foundation in New York provides support services for the homeless, the unemployed, and for AIDS patients. They also offer a kindergarten class for their clients' children. On this day, a kindergarten teacher, in a room full of four- and five-year-olds, watches as Adrianne takes out a box of clay. Pretty soon Adrianne starts throwing small pieces of clay, first on the ground, then against the ceiling, and then at the teacher. The teacher keeps mirroring:*

> *Teacher*: You are throwing a small piece of clay on the ground ... you are throwing a small piece of clay against the ceiling ... and it belongs in the box ... something in you feels like throwing the clay ... now you are throwing a small ball of clay on the cupboard ... and it belongs in the box ... you are throwing the clay at me ... and it belongs in the box ... there is something in you that wants to throw that clay.

> *The kindergarten teacher mirrors with her words the different ways in which Adrian is throwing clay. She also keeps picking up the clay and putting it back in the box. Each time she repeats: "The clay belongs in the box ... I will do that for you." After fewer than three minutes Adrianne puts all the clay in the box, nestles herself in the teacher's lap and gently starts rocking to and fro. A little later she is humming a tune.*

> *Later Adrianne takes the clay out of the box again and starts kneading it. The kindergarten teacher then mirrors the soft feeling of clay in the hand.*

Reflection:

- *Do you recognize the mirroring of actual behavior as well as what the kindergarten teacher suspects is going on inside the little girl?*
- *Do you notice that the teacher assumes that Adrianne knows very well that the clay belongs in the box? She keeps repeating*

this as a casual remark. Without saying it explicitly, she radiates the message: Adrianne will solve this herself.

• *Throughout this communication there is no judgment by the kindergarten teacher. Adrianne knows that throwing clay is not right and disapproval by the teacher won't help the process.*

Mirroring the emotions

Mirroring also works when children show emotions, even intense emotions. You don't have to dry their tears immediately or say: "Please tone down your anger." You can first be with the tears and the anger by offering them back in words: "Your face looks angry and cloudy. Now a whole lot of tears are coming." In this way the child learns to observe his behavior, and see his emotions from some distance. After that, the child can reflect on that which is deeper than the emotion.

Teachers are often afraid of children's emotions. They don't know how to deal with them, especially when intense or dark emotions such as anger or sadness appear. They are afraid that these emotions will become even more intense if they pay attention to them.

While this may be true momentarily, our experience shows that when we give space to an emotion, or are with it in an attentive way, this bodily feeling can be a source of change. When this process of change gets going, the intensity of the external behavior abates.

When you respond by mirroring, the child will probably refine your words. If you understood it wrong, the young person can and will correct you. He gets the chance to search for other words, another expression for what he wants to say. Your response "You seem very sad" might be changed into "No, I am terribly sad," if it fits his inner feeling better. You could even say to the child: "Is it all right if I say you are very sad?" Then you make clear that you don't expect the child automatically to agree with you.

Being open to their correcting you is more important with children than with adults. Adults have an easier time standing up for themselves but children are more dependent on adult intentions. By accepting their words over your own, you let the children know that you hear them until their feelings are clear again. You continue to listen until their story is finished; if the child keeps repeating the same thing, it's because he doesn't think you have heard him.

In a kindergarten in Iceland, listening attentively is the practice among all the teachers. One kindergarten teacher, Ingbörg, is sitting on the ground. Three five-year-olds are playing with large building blocks, building things together and on their own. Ingbörg sits with them, but not in their space. All she does is articulate what the children are doing and she repeats what they say to each other.

Sometimes a conflict arises when two children want to take the same building block. Ingbörg mirrors what she notices about this conflict. Just having her name it helps the children come to a solution on their own. None of the children yell or push and Ingbörg does not have to intervene.

Reflection:
Do you think it would be possible for you to react to children in this way? Simply to give back what they do and say?

Mirroring is more than parroting

Parroting means to repeat what the child says, word for word. Sometimes this leads to reflection in the child, but usually it is insufficient. With mirroring you imagine yourself inside the child's thoughts, perceptions and feelings. You empathize and rephrase. By showing your understanding, or your attempts to understand, you offer something more powerful than parroting.

Outlined below are several kinds of mirroring. You'll notice that they are all different from word-for-word parroting.

Mirroring the essence. Mirroring has a lot to do with choice. It is not literally repeating what the child says, because you go in search of the essence. You ask yourself which words are most important to reflect.

Mirroring the behavior. Children say a lot with their body language. Non-verbal language can also be mirrored, either by giving words to it, or by your posture and gestures. But you need to be careful not to convey judgments in your language. If a child kicks against the kitchen table during breakfast, you might be inclined to react by saying, "You've been kicking the whole time. I can't eat like this." However, this sentence is not mirroring. Instead, it gives a clear message: "I don't want kicking during my breakfast." A mirroring response, by contrast, would merely reflect the child's action: "You're kicking the table with your foot."

Mirroring by summarizing. If the child has a lot to say, it is a good idea to summarize. Sometimes the child bubbles over with language and your summary can give them space. Such mirroring stops the waterfall and helps the child survey the whole picture.

Mirroring the emotional quality. Both behavior and language often give indications of what emotions are bothering the child. Because these emotions are part of their inner experience, it is necessary to proceed with caution. You can't be sure your reading of the emotion is correct, so you should leave room for the child to check your words inside, to see whether or not your mirroring fits. You might say, "It is as if something is angry in your foot."

Mirroring the positive. Mirroring paves the way for change, but repeating all the negative things that the child is doing is more inhibiting than stimulating. Therefore if you have a choice, be sure to mirror what is positive.

Mirroring a visible change. During the conversation there may occur differences in the child's facial expression and posture: shoulders that drop down, a sigh that is released, a smile that comes out. Giving this information back to the child is a form of mirroring. Once again you should avoid articulating either judgment or appreciation. "You look a lot better now" shows appreciation but can meet with resistance a lot quicker than "I see your face isn't frowning as much as before."

Mirroring a discovery. It is so beautiful when a child discovers something new by himself. A personal discovery can act as a great incentive, especially when the child hears you say it back in your mirroring. If the child introduces something new, be sure to mirror it. Parts of a story they've already told, or repetitions of what came before, don't have to be mirrored a second time.

Useful language for mirroring
By using certain sentences you carefully check whether that which you suppose is going on inside the child at this moment actually matches the child's experience. You can say:
> It seems as if ...
> Sometimes there are children who ...
> It seems that there is something inside you that ...
> Something is occurring to me ... I'm wondering if ...?

After an assumption you need to ask yourself, "Is that correct?" It requires some care not to impose your own thinking.

It is best to avoid asking questions when you're mirroring. Statements are much better. Questions demand answers and change a child's train of thought. Statements leave more space for a child to stay with his story.

In class Laura talks about her weekend with her grandparents. The teacher notices that both Laura's words and her body language indicate how exciting it was, a whole weekend without her parents. The teacher asks a question: "Laura, was that exciting for you?" Laura can only answer "yes" or "no." It sounds very different if the teacher makes a statement: "Laura, that was exciting!"

Over time, once the child becomes used to mirroring, listening in this way will create a bond between the two of you. Mirroring instills a sense of safety. It is non-threatening. The child perceives that you are listening, and feels free to develop her own thoughts and feelings.

In a day-care center Amber, 2 years old, is sucking on a long string from her blouse. There is a knot at the end of it. The teacher Carrie is afraid that she will swallow the string. It seems plausible that if Carrie were to say: "Amber ... do not chew on that string ... that is dangerous ... take it out of your mouth" Carrie could pull the string out of Amber's mouth and say: "Good girl, now go and play again." Carrie would be satisfied that she had noticed dangerous behavior and prevented Amber from choking on the string.

But how would Amber experience this? Can you imagine what the effect of these words would be? It is possible that Amber would think:

- *Adults know how it is supposed to be done and I don't.*
- *I must obey and do what other people tell me, because that is when they like me.*
- *Something I like is wrong. It is not allowed.*
- *Carrie thinks I'm stupid because I suck on a string.*

In reality Carrie reacted very differently:
Carrie: Amber what do you have in your mouth?
Carrie touches her own mouth as if she is feeling it herself. Amber takes the piece of string out of her mouth and looks at it.
Carrie: Oh I see a long piece of string there ... can I have a look? What is that piece of string like?
Amber looks at the piece of string together with Carrie.
Carrie: It has become wet ... it is a really long piece of string ... it is from your blouse, isn't it?
Amber puts it in her mouth again.
Carrie: The string from your blouse ... and you like it in your mouth.
Amber: Out ...

She pulls the string out of her mouth.
Carrie: You take it out ... out of your mouth is better, isn't it?
Amber climbs down from her chair, looks at the other children and moves in their direction to go and play again.

Reflection:
 • *Do you recognize "you like it in your mouth" as the most important mirroring because Amber feels acknowledged in her feelings?*
 • *Do you notice the difference between the two scenarios?*
 • *What kind of influence do you think the actual interaction has on Amber's development?*

At first mirroring may sound unnatural. The children can react uncomfortably, protesting "But I just said that." If this happens, simply explain your intention concerning mirroring. Explain that you want to see if you understand. Or ask for their help with a "mirroring experiment." Children will be more than willing to give it a try.

Children can listen to others
Not only adults, but children also can learn to listen in this empathic manner. Children acquire listening skills in two ways: "model learning" and "the law of effect."

First, children learn how to listen from models in their environment, primarily their family, and later, their teacher. Children their own age also have a major influence, but basically, the way in which an adult listens to a child determines how the child listens.

To what extent does a teacher half-listen, while busy with ten other things? To what degree does a child-care provider listen attentively? Listening adults create listening children.

Another way of learning is from the law of effect. Children learn from the reactions of others. If a child does his utmost to listen to his teacher, her reaction determines whether he will repeat this action in the future. If listening is never rewarded, this behavior will decrease sharply. If the teacher reacts only when the child talks loudly, the child will learn that talking loudly is more effective than listening.

Children can learn to mirror each other. With very young children, mirroring sometimes does start off as simple parroting in which children repeat whole sentences word for word. Over time and with training, the parroting is refined, and children learn to listen carefully and mirror back what they hear on a deeper level.

Mirroring requires their intense concentration. Because of this, it actively involves children in each other's stories. The child who is telling her story is positively affected by the intense listening and the reflections of the other children which help her clarify her own inner sensing.

9

The Focusing Attitude

There is one basic condition to helping a child focus, and that is that you must develop the basic Focusing attitude. Being accepting of your inner self allows you to accept that of a child. Be sure that you stay with your felt sense as you invite him to do the same. As he speaks, listen closely and acceptingly, just the way you would want to listen to your own felt sense.

Along with your acceptance of your own inner experience, there are a few other concepts basic to the Focusing attitude.

Being friendly and trusting to what is there

You need to trust that children have their own inner wisdom. Your desire is to help them to discover it. When you can be friendly to whatever comes inside you, you can help children be friendly to whatever comes inside them. You help them say to themselves, "Hello there, nice child."

Keeping the right distance

You also need to stay at the right distance. You do not want to impose or force yourself on a child. You ask the child's permission at each step of the way. Because you trust that the child has an inner sense of rightness, you can trust that Focusing is occurring anyway, even if you do not get a visible reaction from the child.

Keeping talk to a minimum

In line with keeping yourself at the right distance, you keep your talk to a minimum. When you do talk, you use neutral non-judgmental language. You may be curious, but you do not delve into the content of what the child says.

Respecting a child's privacy

In the Focusing process, you are facilitating the child's entry into a deeper, more sensitive area that only she can access. It is an area best explored in silence — just the child and her inner world. It is especially important to respect a child's privacy at this time. In that inner place, every child is especially sensitive to anything that feels like pressure or coercion. You can't and don't have to know exactly what is going on inside her.

It may help to ask yourself now and then whether you are "with" the child or, even better, a small step behind. You don't need to know exactly where the child is at every moment, but you need to be quietly attentive, and respectful. At first, the flow of the Focusing process may seem unclear. But with practice, it will feel easy and natural.

> *Marta asks a colleague about her experiences using Focusing at school. The colleague reflects for a little while and doesn't come up with more than "good." But as she continues to talk, she recalls one experience after another. At the end of the conversation, she says: "I didn't know what to say at first. Focusing has become so interwoven in my attitude that I don't experience it as special any more. But as I was talking, I started thinking of all the subtle changes in the children that have resulted."*

Honoring "no"

Part of the Focusing attitude is to recognize and respect that a child might not want to focus. It is not easy, in all your enthusiasm, to be confronted with a "no" when you believe you have the child's best interests at heart. Yet, when the child makes it clear that he isn't ready to bring his attention inside, you respect that. It doesn't mean that he will never want to focus with you. It does mean that he knows that, at this moment, he doesn't want to do it. That clarity alone merits your absolute respect.

A child may say "no" explicitly, but it is also possible that he will communicate in guarded terms, or use non-verbal ways to indicate a boundary that he doesn't want you to cross. If the conversation stops suddenly or if the child changes the subject, these may be clues that focusing is not welcome at that moment. You might hear or see some of the following:

"Look, there's a bird flying."
"I hear the ambulance."
The child takes a toy and walks away.
The child goes very quiet and motionless.
While you are talking, the child starts to kick a ball.

It can be helpful to offer mirroring in these moments, because then you make their communication explicit: "We were just talking about the fight with your friend, about where you feel that. Now you see that bird flying ... maybe you don't want to continue about the fight with your friend ... You are showing me that maybe you don't want to talk about it now ... and that is okay with me."

You can also invite the child to listen to that "no" inside: ... "Do you notice anywhere inside that wants to say 'no'? What is that like for you?" Depending on the situation, the following can happen:

The child feels encouraged to continue thinking and talking about the fight with the friend.

The "no" feels understood and justified and the conversation about the fight ends.

The child checks inside. Maybe something there feels as if it can't be said.

Children can also say "no" to protect themselves. They may not wish to relive a painful experience. The "no" that arises inside may indicate that something isn't ready or doesn't feel right, even if the child doesn't know why.

> *Anna is a withdrawn fifteen-year-old girl. She is sensitive to bullying but does not defend herself or ask for help when she needs it. Counselor Gonda suggests that she attend a social skills training.*
>
> *Anna*: Stop harping on that. I am not going to do that training anyway ...
>
> *Gonda*:There is something in you that says "no" ... No, to the idea of going to someone for help ... And no to participating in this training ...
>
> *Anna*: It's just like in elementary school. Whenever I spoke up about being bullied, the teacher would tell me off just as badly as the kid who was bullying me.
>
> *Gonda*:Just like in elementary school ... you also got told off ... something in you assumes the same thing will happen again

These words prove to be a turning point in the session. An old situation has been heard and the pressure around it is eased. A little later Anna agrees to do the training.

"I'm so sad alone in my bed."

Reflection:

> *Gonda mirrored what she assumed was happening inside Anna. Something inside Anna was protecting her from having another hurtful experience. But once the fear of losing face had been heard, Anna was able do something about it.*

Things that are preferable not to say or do

Focusing is a very free, open practice, but there are some behaviors which are antithetical to the basic Focusing attitude. Your Focusing will probably be more successful if you observe the following cautions:

- Avoid offering advice, interpretation or judgment. This means neither condemning *nor* praising the child while focusing.
- Avoid knowing better, even for the other person's good.
- Be careful with comforting. Remember that comforting can also block the child's own ability to solve problems.
- Don't let a child lose face; never embarrass her in the presence of others.
- Don't ask for details of a situation.
- Don't ask "why."
- Don't add anything to what the child herself has said.
- Avoid action words. For example, rather than saying, "Try to find a word or image," you can say, "Allow a word or image to come up."
- Avoid the words "try," "maybe," "for a little while," "think."
- Don't answer with "yes but." "Yes but" amounts to the same thing as "no."
- Avoid the words "always" and "never."
- Avoid haste.
- Don't plan your responses in advance. Wait until a response comes from inside you.
- Finally, take care to change your pronouns. When you mirror someone, the "I" becomes "you."

How discouraging it must be for children when adults always know better! Adults are often inclined to steer the direction of the conversation, to offer advice. What goes on inside the child then? If the child gets the message that the adult decides it all anyway, what is the point of him examining it on his own? If he internalizes this message, that adults know best, much of his inner knowing is lost.

Limits as to time and safety

Of course, teachers need to control behavior and to enforce rules. The teacher needs to decide what the children should or shouldn't do. You need to be firm when it comes to setting limits to time or safety. Notice that you make a distinction between allowing feelings and allowing certain behaviors; you accept emotions but you also observe the limits.

It makes a big difference if, in certain situations, you and the child decide together about what will happen, either in class or at home.

Acceptance

What is meant by acceptance? As you have seen, it is not the same as accepting behavior. You can accept a child's wishes and desires without accepting his behavior.

Often "acceptance" is viewed as something passive, as not doing anything about a difficult child or situation. Yet taking time to be with a child, and allowing them their internal freedom, is an active decision that does not happen on its own.

It is thought that if you accept a child, it is not necessary for you to show it. However, it is not enough that a teacher feels she accepts a problem child in her class. While acceptance starts from within, it only works if it is visible from the outside, by the child. The child decides through the teacher's behavior and language whether real acceptance is present.

Acceptance starts from *being there.* This also sounds passive, but *being there* is actually rare and can have great significance. By *being there* we mean that, while you are there, children can go ahead with what they are doing, secure in knowing that someone is observing closely. You don't interfere in the process, but you do pay attention.

A teacher has tried everything possible to solve arguments for the children. Now he finds through Focusing that it is enough for him to be present. He does not have to come running with solutions. The children in his class develop their own strategies for dealing with arguments. All he has to do is to voice his observations, and not voice anything else.

Daring to be still

Daring to be still is part of acceptance. Allowing long pauses says a lot about trust in communication. It says that you trust the child will come up with her own solutions.

Donald's daughter, Jane, is almost four years old. Jane has set her heart on eating two muffins. Jane wants two muffins in her hands and she wants them now. She pulls out all the stops to achieve this.

Both parents look at each other: how are we going to solve this one? If we give in, she will learn that pitching a fit gets results. However, it is also touching to see how much Jane wants those muffins. Donald and his wife love her so much that they want to give her everything!

Nevertheless they stay strong and hold their ground: "We know that you really want to have two muffins, but one is enough for you. Your tummy really wants two muffins, because they taste so good, but still we are only giving you one."

At this point, instead of saying more, Jane's parents pause and allow her room to absorb the situation. Then Jane reacts: "I know! If I break that one muffin in two, then I will also have two."

She beams at her smart solution and then she enjoys "her two muffins."

Reflection:

The girl finds the solution without her parents' help. Doing so gives her confidence and increases her capacity to problem-solve. Would you have been able to make up such a solution yourself?

Communication with respectful silence allows everyone to be self-reflective. If you can build some silent time into your contact with children, they will seek ideas and answers inside themselves. When you are always talking, there is the chance that the child will not feel accepted and communication will die out.

Once you listen to what children say — receiving their words without judgment or interpretation — children adopt an independent attitude quickly. Learning that their own thinking and perception are listened to and appreciated, children take a further step towards self-reliance. They accept boundaries, but in time the boundaries are mostly from within and not because another person says so.

Practice this in the next couple of days: When children come to you with a problem, don't offer any solution. Take an attentive and neutral attitude. Let the children search for decisions and solutions themselves. Just be with them, reflecting the problem. You will be pleased by the result.

Presence

Another way to *be there* is to have *presence.* That is, when you listen to the child, you are present with your whole being. Thoughts about what you have to do are cast aside for a while. You fully concentrate on whatever the child wants to be with.

If you simply can't be present because you have to talk to someone else, grade papers, etc., then arrange a time later when you are able to give the child undisturbed attention. By making a clear-cut agreement about when there will be time for you and the child, you avoid shallow contacts. Children can go their own way and take care of themselves, especially if they know that they will have your attention later. Just make sure they do have your total attention for those special moments.

Being present implies a type of neutrality on your part. You let each child be the expert on his own life. Neutrality avoids the dangers of judging, disapproving or "knowing best." It means letting your own needs and wishes go for the moment and creating a neutral space in which the child can develop.

Presence also requires empathy, which means that as you follow the child's story you imagine what is going on in his or her life, getting your own felt sense of it.

10

Children's Symbols

Symbolizing is the child's equivalent of finding a handle with which to hold on to their felt sense. It allows him to sustain a connection. As he symbolizes, the felt sense gets clearer, and the child adjusts his symbols to suit what is happening inside.

Drawing, painting, working with clay or even movement can all give expression to a felt sense. Sometimes words come, but they are not always necessary. Change can occur even if there are no words to describe it. When you see that a child is in contact with a felt sense, invite her to draw from it. That is the easiest form of symbolizing. Ask her which colors go along with that experience, what kinds of movement her hand wants to make on the paper. When there are many different feelings, drawing allows the child to see them all on paper and gain a little perspective.

> *At a campsite in Hungary a mother is busy with her two-year-old deaf child. Her other son Marc is constantly angry. He is currently throwing a tantrum, totally out of control, and his mother is at her wit's end. She asks Marta for help. Marta sits down at the picnic table near Marc.*
>
> *Marta*: Phew, you are angry … Where is all this anger inside sitting? … here? (*She points to his belly*) Here? (*She points to his chest*) (*Handing him pen and paper*) Just let your hand make all that anger on the paper.
>
> *Marc draws a few round and diagonal lines.*
>
> *Marta*: Is there still more anger that wants to come out on the paper?

Marc starts another drawing. On the second paper his hand dares to express more. He puts this paper aside and starts on a third piece of paper. His face has gotten red and he is drawing with extreme concentration. This third drawing is even bigger and more complex than the others. Marc grips the pen and pushes down hard. Then he stops and breathes a sigh of relief.

Reflection:

• *Through these three drawings Marc symbolizes his anger. Doing so allows him to relax. It is surprising that he uses three different sheets of paper. Most children continue on the same piece of paper. Can you follow the renewed process in each drawing?*

• *Marta shows Marc's mother how her son can express his anger in a way that helps him feel understood. His deaf brother gets a lot of the attention in their family. Possibly, if Marc feels heard, he might not need to rely on his rebellious behavior.*

• *Marta does not interpret these drawings. There are no fixed symbols, such as the crown of a tree standing for thinking, or the roots standing for the will. The drawings stand for an experience far subtler than words can express, and can only be interpreted by the child.*

Occasionally a child may resist the creative tools you offer. This could be because he is worried about not doing it right. If this is the case, assure him that whatever he creates doesn't have to be happy or pretty. You can even take a little time to listen to the part inside of him that feels pressured to "do it right." Taking this mini-step may liberate the child from the feeling.

Symbols work when they fit a child's experienced feeling exactly. Then they free the child up inside, giving him more space to grow and develop. When you focus with a child, you will notice that often what comes is very different from what you expected.

Symbols come in different forms:

drawing	painting
crafts	telling the inner story out loud
writing	playing or acting
clay sculptures	movement and sound

Drawing

Even outside the context of Focusing, drawing (as well as other creative mediums) is frequently used to help children process emotional experiences. The Jewish Museum in Prague includes a revealing collection of drawings by Bosnian children expressing the trauma of war. Artistic expression can be extremely valuable in helping children communicate some of their experiences so that the trauma doesn't take over inside, drowning out everything else.

Drawing is a simple and powerful way to help children contact a felt sense. As they draw, they can feel something forming inside and they can also feel when a new direction begins to announce itself. They need never talk about what happened or make the content of their difficult experiences explicit. In fact, a very complete and healing process can take place without the children ever sharing the meaning of what they are exploring.

> *Simon*: Sometimes I can just sit for an hour.
> *Marta*: Just sit for an hour ... with nothing moving.
> *Simon*: I just sit like this.
> *Marta*: Just sit and wait ... what kind of feeling does that bring?
> *Simon*: A nice feeling ... I am sitting so peacefully ...
> *Simon's expression is dreamy.*
> *Marta*: As if you are getting dreamy ...
> *Simon*: Yes ...
> *Marta*: Does that feeling ... what does it look like? ... for example does it look like cotton?
> *Simon*: No ... more like clouds.
> *Marta*: Do those clouds have a color?
> *Simon*: Yellow.
> *Marta*: Could you draw that, just sitting and waiting? ...
> *Simon draws very intensely; he looks up after some time.*
> *Simon*: Do you know what I made? There is a dog that you see in the clouds ... ears, tail, head ... *(Simon continues to draw)* There is more ... there's another dog ... and more clouds.
> *Marta*: Even more clouds, another dog ...
> *Simon*: Like this ... *(Simon continues drawing)*
> *Marta*: All in the clouds ...
> *Simon*: Here they are ... do you get it?
> *Marta*: Does it have something to say?
> *Simon*: It is a dog, a cat and a mouse.
> *Marta*: It is a dog, a cat and a mouse ... they are in your clouds ...
> *Simon*: Yes, the dog is first ... he chases the cat ... and the cat goes after the mouse.
> *Marta*: Oh yes, that is the way it is with those clouds inside you ...
> *Simon*: Oooh.
> *Marta*: The mouse ... and that is what those clouds do inside. They want to catch each other.

Simon: The dog chases the cat ... the cat chases the mouse ...

Marta: Just like something keeps chasing you inside ...

Simon gestures, making a circle with his right hand.

Simon: And so on and so on.

Marta makes the same motion with her hand.

Marta: Can you put that on paper too?

Simon draws the circular movements.

Marta: Inside you everyone runs after someone else ... That's how that goes ... And it goes on and on.

Simon draws, concentrating intensely.

Marta: And do they always chase each other the same way or ... also the other way around?

Simon: Wait a moment ... *(Simon pauses for a moment, starts to write and then reads out loud)* Bowwow! Meow! Peep ...

Marta: What kind of peep is this?

Simon: *(producing a kind of anxious peep)* Peeeeep ... This is a scared peep. The cat is scared of the dog and the mouse is afraid of the cat.

Marta: That's what goes with the scared feeling inside. They are chasing each other ... the one scared thing is chasing the other scared thing ...

Simon: Look, the dog wants to bite the cat ... and the cat wants to eat the mouse.

Marta: The dog wants to bite the cat ... and the cat wants to eat the mouse ... and all that is in your cloud ...

Simon: Yes ... all that.

Reflection:

• *Later, Marta learns from Simon's mother that a dog jumped on him when he was a baby. Ever since then, Simon has avoided dogs. He is particularly afraid of his neighbor's big dog. To his mother's great surprise, after therapy, Simon walked straight up to the neighbor's dog. He started to play with it and even hung on its neck. Simon did not mention any of this to Marta, but his mother noticed the change and passed it on.*

• *Do you notice how 'illogically' Simon's inner story unfolds? He speaks almost incoherently about clouds, a dog, a cat and a mouse. Where is it all coming from? Fear of animals is never discussed. The felt sense of Simon's cloud carries a lot of meaning for him, and step-by-step, that meaning is symbolized. Afterwards the logic of it can be understood.*

Marta has used drawing and painting with children in various continents. She notices that children of all ages and nationalities welcome the chance to draw something from inside them and that the technique can be used to address a wide range of issues.

> *Greta, a teacher in Holland who has taught the ten-year-olds in her class how to focus, notices that Peter is unusually quiet and withdrawn one morning. He is having a hard time concentrating on his work.*
>
> *Greta*: Peter, you are so quiet this morning. You haven't started working.
>
> *Peter*: My neighbor is getting buried today. He was my friend. We used to go fishing together and he taught me how to catch fish. He just suddenly died.
>
> *Peter starts to cry.*
>
> *Greta*: Where inside do you feel all that, about your neighbor's death?
>
> *Peter points to his stomach and huddles up a little.*
>
> *Greta*: There in your stomach and you huddle up. Could you ask inside how that feeling wants to be drawn or colored? And will you draw what comes up from inside?
>
> *With a black pen, Peter starts to draw in his Focusing sketchbook. The teacher once again turns her attention to the group. Meanwhile Peter draws his own house and that of the neighbors. He also draws a fishing rod with a fish on it and a coffin. His tears subside and a deep sigh follows. A smile appears through his tears. A little later he begins his schoolwork. The rest of the morning he works steadily. During the lunch break, Greta takes the opportunity of talking together about the drawing.*
>
> *Greta*: Does your drawing have something to say?
>
> *Now Peter calmly talks about his neighbor's death and funeral. He explains that his drawing expresses how much he misses him. Greta asks Peter what it feels like inside now that he has drawn all that. Peter says that there is room again in his stomach. Greta asks whether this "room" also has a color, and if he wants to draw it on paper.*
>
> *Peter chooses a red pen and moves his hand now in circles across the page. With this method he strengthens the feeling of "more room" inside.*

Reflection:

• *Do you notice the change that Peter symbolizes in the second drawing? The heavy pressing feeling has disappeared and he can breathe again.*

• *It's a good idea to have a short talk with the child after a Focusing session. If you can't speak with the child right away, that's OK. Know that the child will continue to process the experience on his own.*

Remind children that they can draw both pleasant and unpleasant feelings. Pleasant feelings are also strengthened by giving attention to them. The children can keep these feelings longer. Bad feelings are strengthened at first by giving attention to them, but then they diminish and disappear. The child feels better, more spacious or light inside.

It is handy if every child has his own focusing sketchbook in class. This book is very personal and the teacher makes sure that it stays that way. This sketchbook is kept in the classroom until the end of the school year.

Painting

The great thing about painting is that it invites more and more to come. Children can express themselves by mixing and smearing colors and lines like modern painters. Pre-schoolers can use finger paint as in the example right. As with any artistic tool, paint needn't be used to create realistic scenes.

> *In a class of four- and five-year-olds at the Greyston Foundation in Yonkers, New York, Gayle leads a group of fourteen children in clearing a space. Then, with her two assistants, Gayle places two large pieces of paper on the floor.*
>
> *Gayle suggests that the children check inside. "What is your safe color?" she asks. She invites the children to paint with their safe color. They apply it with their fingers. At first they paint in small spaces very near themselves. After a little while their movements become expansive and the colors spread out and blend together.*
>
> *Next Gayle asks, "Is there something angry or scared inside? What color is that?"*
>
> *The children all choose different colors. They move their hands quickly and the colors are very intense. The children are deep in concentration. When they are finished, they follow the example of Gayle's assistants and call out, "This is the angry color ... This is the scared color ..."*

After washing their hands they all sit in the circle. Gayle says, "Close your eyes ... feel your feet on the ground ... what is it like inside now?" In one voice the children call out: "Happy!" Gayle affirms this collective feeling by leading the group in a familiar song:

"Hands up, Give me your heart. Put your hands up. Give me your love, All your lo-o-o-ve"

As the song instructs, the children put their hands above their heads and then place them on their hearts. They sway to and fro, repeating the song several times.

Reflection:

Notice that a sense of safety is established first. Only after they feel safe are the children invited to contact their darker feelings. Many of the children at the Greyston Foundation come from troubled families. If they had been instructed to begin by exploring their difficult feelings, it might have been overwhelming. Instead, the whole atmosphere is characterized by a feeling of wellness and safety, even as the children explore anger or fear.

For adolescents in particular, abstract painting can be very freeing. It affords them a measure of privacy, and can seem more adult than drawing pictures. The activity can continue until everything has been expressed, and the young person is liberated for the moment from everything that was in his way. At the same time — and for some young people this is a relief — no feelings at all have to come. The young person can still paint or draw. And since painting and drawing are kinetic activities, they help loosen the body, and with the body, stuck feelings are loosened also.

The person can also refrain from painting. A blank canvas is a perfectly satisfactory expression that nothing wants to be shown right now.

Joachim is a thirteen-year-old with ADHD. His parents have divorced and it feels to him as though his whole world has collapsed.

He paints with several colors, letting them flow into each other. Then he takes the largest brush and, with careful strokes, covers the entire paper with black paint. His therapist is startled by how dark the image is. He is tempted to say something like, "Surely it can't be that bad. After all, you can still play football and tennis, right?" But he knows that to say this would violate Joachim's reality. Instead he stays close to Joachim's process, mirroring: "Everything is covered in black."

Joachim stops painting for a while and kicks a ball around in a corner of the room. Then he returns, paints a thin line of yellow and then paints over the entire black surface with bright red. It's as if something new has a chance to be expressed. He looks at his painting and says in an unusually soft voice: "That's that. Shall we play chess now?"

Reflection:

In this sequence, the therapist's only action is to mirror Joachim. It seems that the less you do as a Focusing companion, the more can happen in the child.

Working with clay

When you have a serious conversation with a child, who does most of the talking? Does the conversation embarrass her? Does she become antagonistic? What would happen if next time, you just offered her a lump of clay and asked her to do with it whatever her hands wanted? What would happen if you invited her to use the clay to express what she was feeling inside?

Eddie is twelve years old. Every week he meets with a remedial teacher to work on his aggression. Each week she asks, "Can you check how it is inside today?" And she offers him a lump of clay. Eddie's hands take over, sculpting forms that express what he feels inside. He asks his teacher not to tell anyone what he's made. After each session he returns the clay to a big round ball.

One day, Eddie sculpts several snakes. He asks his teacher to make something too. He says it doesn't matter what. She begins to sculpt a form, which Eddie takes to be a baby. "The snakes come to eat the baby, and everything becomes crap," he says. He makes dozens of balls of crap. The teacher makes more and more babies. Eddie gets very excited when the snakes eat up the babies and everything becomes crap. His teacher asks what's happening inside him when the snakes eat the baby. Breathless, Eddie replies, "It hurts very, very much." The teacher mirrors how bad the baby feels, how dangerous it is when the snakes come and eat it up, and then there's all that crap. She repeats this using many different words and tones of voice. After several sessions devoted to this theme, the baby gets a cradle and the snakes protect the baby.

Slowly, Eddie's behavior changes.

Reflection:

Notice how the clay invites creativity. For Eddie, as for countless other children, expressing the felt sense furthers his ability to deal with it, to allow it to change, and eventually to change his behavior.

Using crafts to build a safe space

One way to use crafts in Focusing is to build a safe space. You start by assembling an appealing pile of shoeboxes, egg crates, colorful construction paper, ribbons and feathers, as well as scissors and glue. Then invite a group of children to construct a safe space, where they can leave their worries and problems. As they build, invite them to check inside whether their structures are just right or whether something needs to be added. You'll be amazed at what they create: castles, rockets, and mountaintops. The children's energy and attention during this process will be very different than it is during a regular craft project. Their concentration will be deeper and it will have a quality of emotional engagement.

With her parents' help, Christine uses Focusing to make a castle where she stores her worries. For her tenth birthday, her parents propose that she make another such structure with her friends. Her mother offers to teach her friends how to clear a space inside. On the day of the birthday party, the children design and build, tinker and decorate. They write notes and draw pictures, articulating and depicting their worries. They place all of these inside the structure. Afterwards they talk about the experience. There is a calm feeling in the room, and the children are kind and attentive to one another. When she goes to bed that evening, Christine reflects, "I'm glad my friends know how to clear a space inside now too."

Reflection:

Focusing can be an individual or a shared experience among children.

Telling the inner story

When you are a focusing companion, you are of course inviting the child to tell you his inner story. It is easy to assume you know exactly what he feels and speak to that. But this is a mistake. The most helpful thing you can do is to let the child's internal feeling speak for itself, and tell its own story.

Seven-year-old Esmée approaches Marta.

Esmée: We are getting another baby at home.

Marta tries not to show her enthusiasm, She doesn't say "How nice for you!" Then Marta would be speaking for the girl and Marta doesn't know whether the girl likes the idea of a baby or not. Mirroring helps her stay in contact with Esmée and allows Esmée the opportunity to carry her own process forward.

Marta: Yes, you are getting another baby, aren't you?

Esmée shrugs her shoulders.

Esmée: I don't want a little brother.

Here too, Marta could react from all she knows about families and convince Esmée that having a little brother will be lots of fun. But something about the way Esmée says this puts Marta on the alert. What could Esmée mean? Marta mirrors the child's words and asks a question, inviting her to get the felt sense of the whole situation.

Marta: You don't want a little brother ... Can you notice anywhere inside that does not want a little brother?

With a wide gesture of her hand, Esmée points to an area high in her chest. Marta moves her hand in the same way. Esmée understands this as an invitation to proceed.

Esmée: Boys are always so rough.

She tenses her shoulders.

Marta: Always those rough boys ... *(also tensing her shoulders)*

Esmée: Yes, because when I walk into the schoolyard those big boys are playing football so wildly I can't even get past them to where my friends are. I don't dare walk past.

Marta: You are scared to cross the schoolyard when boys are playing football.

Esmée: But I can also do this ... *(And now she pulls a "nobody is going to push me around" face, straightens her shoulders and takes a few big steps)* Then they don't scream at me and I am already on the other side.

Marta: If you cross like that, then you'll be fine. You can feel it when you straighten your shoulders like that.

Reflection:

• *How would you react to a girl who told you she didn't want a little brother? No one could have predicted that inside Esmée linked getting a little brother to the wild play of the boys in the schoolyard.*

• *Focusing doesn't have to be more than this. Do you notice that by the end, Esmée has more room for the arrival of a little brother?*

Writing

Symbolizing by writing is not a common thing in young children. Most children link writing to schoolwork, and prefer something easier, such as coloring. Yet there are children who use writing as a handle for the felt sense.

Some children write a long story. Others use just a few words. Keeping in touch with their inner experience makes it a Focusing story, not a fantasy story. Some will give their work a title that captures the whole of it, like: "Everything that is Bothering Patricia." Others, like the following boy, write something like a poem.

"When Mommy is not there,
Feeling bored in the square.
Bullying kids,
Running into the teacher and
principal,
Am as angry as a horse."

als mama er niet is.
vervelen op het plein.
kinderen peten.
begon alle mester enjuffrouw oplopen
ben zo boos als een paard.

As a teacher you may wonder how to deal with writing errors. The best thing to do is to distinguish between your role as teacher and your role as Focusing companion. Assure the child that during this time, spelling and grammar are not important.

Movement and sound

Children often express their energy and relieve aggression through sports. While this relief of tension can be helpful, sports do not express what wants to be heard inside. Children can be guided to express their inner experience in sound and movement. You can ask them, when they are having difficult feelings, which movement or sound would feel right.

Laura is a teacher at a Special Education school in Hungary. For the last nine months she has practiced clearing a space with a group of eight six and seven-year olds. At any time of the day when the children feel overwhelmed, a space is made for Focusing. The class has evolved from a tangle of uncontrollable kids to a considerate group of children who are attentive to each other and able to concentrate. During Focusing time, Andrew draws blue and green lines on his sheet of paper. Afterwards, Laura asks if any of the drawings have something to say. While Andrew speaks, his classmate, Peter, listens attentively.

Andrew: I am still very angry because this morning Peter bullied me when we were with the other teacher.

Laura: You are very angry ... Peter bullied you ... Where do you feel all that bullying?

Andrew:In my head ... here ... and I have to cry and I want my Mommy.

Laura notices that more attention is required. She asks the other children to occupy themselves, so that Andrew can have room for his angry feeling.

Laura: It is in your head ... you have to cry ... and you want to go to your mother. Can you ask inside what "it" wants to do, in order to get the angry part out?

Andrew closes his eyes and listens inside.

Andrew:My leg wants to stamp it out.

Laura: Your leg wants to stamp it out ... Can you ask your leg how it wants to do that?

Andrew:Stamp on something ...

Laura: Can you find something to stamp on?

Andrew takes an aluminum mug from the drawer. He stamps on the mug, making guttural sounds. Laura stays with him, mirroring his movements and feelings.

Laura: You can check inside to see whether all the anger has come out.

Andrew needs a second mug and stamps with both feet, one after the other. Peter watches calmly. Other children come and observe calmly, with interest. Then Andrew smiles. He looks around and asks if he can paint the squashed mugs.

Peter retrieves the second mug and a little later they are standing side by side painting harmoniously.

Reflection:

• *By moving his legs, Andrew symbolizes what his anger wants to express. His body knows when it is enough. Do you notice again how the child is in control of the process? Andrew was able to solve his problem without help from his mother or Laura. Laura only offered options that he could choose.*

• *Peter is a boy who has received a lot of Focusing attention in the past. In this instance he was able to experience the effect of his aggression.*

Playing

Finally, children express their inner being through playing. When you observe play that seems meaningful, you calmly allow it to take its course. Reflect out loud what you see. By mirroring you can help the children penetrate more deeply into whatever needs to be expressed.

A curious inner story develops in the playroom with Werner. When Werner was just over a year old, his grandparents assumed custody of him, because life with his parents was no longer safe. Since then he has been raised by his grandparents. Werner, now eight years old, is playing with a baby doll. He skulks around the room clutching the doll to him, as if he were a thief. He speaks loudly.

Werner: The baby has been stolen! The baby has been stolen!

He paces around, distraught.

Marta: The baby has been stolen ... the baby cannot understand that.

Werner: No, you can't do that ... *(He stamps his foot,)*

Marta: No, this is not okay with the baby ...

Each time he sees Marta, he repeats this scenario. Each time he is calmer. His grandparents report that he is calmer at home too, and no longer wakes up from nightmares.

Reflection:

Do you notice that Marta does not interpret? She does not clarify what the game is about. The symbolizing need only make sense to Werner. Just expressing his felt sense and having it heard allows it to diminish.

11

Introducing Focusing into Different Settings

Around the world, in schools, families, and an array of social institutions, children are Focusing. Focusing happens in many different ways in many different contexts. This chapter is to give you a sense of that range and demonstrate how Focusing can be introduced into these different settings.

Who focuses with children? Family members, of course. (See Chapter 12, *Especially For Parents,* pp. 126–138.) In day-care centers, teachers and paraprofessionals use it. In schools, classroom teachers, remedial teachers, counselors, speech therapists and administrators apply it. In child welfare organizations, group leaders and caseworkers use it. In health care settings, pediatricians, nurses and physical therapists find it helpful. Finally Focusing adds a useful dimension to play therapy and art therapy, indeed to all child psychotherapy.

Adults who use basic Focusing skills notice positive changes, not only in themselves and the children, but also throughout the entire environment where Focusing occurs. They report that it is a relief to communicate with each other when the Focusing attitude is the basis of this work. Because Focusing fosters confidence and respect, it is easier for everyone to weather irritations and resolve disagreements as they arise. Teachers and other professionals can relax their control since, once familiar with Focusing, children are better at solving problems — even preventing them.

In a class where the children have learned to focus as a group, one boy is becoming agitated over a problem he is unable to solve. One of his friends walks up to the teacher and says: "Excuse me, you'd better let Karim do a Focusing drawing because he's getting all red in the face ..." Karim accepts the teacher's invitation and, by drawing in his Focusing notebook, he is able to calm down. Not only is Karim relieved, so are the other children.

As in this example, children can focus, not only with your support, but independently as well. Many children will be able to clear a space, or make contact with a felt sense and draw it, all on their own. They will even be able to do so in difficult circumstances.

WHEN CAN YOU START?

If you're under the impression that you need to immerse yourself in study before starting this program, think again! The first time you focus, especially with children, it can be short and simple, only a matter of three questions:

> *Can I ask you ... where do you feel that in your body? ... How does it feel there? ... What does it want to say? ...*

This is the shortest of Focusing interventions, and it is both simple and effective. In the following example, an introductory workshop leads to immediate results even for a child with a serious problem.

> *In a three-hour workshop in Suriname, Marta trains fourteen counselors to focus with the physically and emotionally abused children in their care. She begins by listening to the participants as they describe a crushing workload and the emotional strain of working with traumatized children. With their approval, Marta asks them to feel inside and invite a felt sense to form.*
>
> *After they have brought their attention inside, Marta asks where in their bodies they feel this heavy workload and the tension of working with traumatized children. They put their hands on their bodies, each on their own spot ... They stay with it with their attention ... A word or an image comes up ... They check whether this fits with the felt sense inside ... A number of them experience a shift ... They receive that and savor it ... They also notice what still needs attention, what they can return to later ... Slowly their eyes open ...*
>
> *After some initial hesitation, a few counselors express how surprised they are by the shift inside.*
>
> *Next, Marta proposes a role-play, in which one of the counselors plays the part of a child and Marta plays the counselor who uses Focusing. Hortance, an experienced counselor, volunteers. She wants to play the role of Ronald, a nine-year-old with a history of sexual abuse by two boys. He has a great need to suck. At times he is completely out of it, sucking intensely on his shirt, pulling at it, and salivating all over it.*
>
> *The role-play takes place on the floor. Hortance, playing the part of Ronald, backs away from Marta.*
>
> *Marta*: You are moving a bit further away ... Can you check inside to find where you would like to sit?
> *Hortance moves closer and sucks on her shirt.*
> *Marta*: You are coming a bit closer ... does it feel right like that?
> *Hortance nods vaguely and looks at Marta expectantly.*

Marta: Your mouth is feeling how it is sucking on your shirt ...
Hortance nods ...
Marta: I will give you a crayon. Could your hand color how that feels inside?
After some hesitation, Hortance starts to draw. Marta continues to describe the actions. More and more colors appear until Hortance puts down the crayon with a sigh.

Hortance is surprised. She reports that she had a profound experience in which she gained some insight into Ronald's inner reality. By drawing the felt sense, she felt a shift inside.

A few weeks later Hortance sends Marta the following email:

The other children exclude Ronald because they think his sucking is dirty. They also react to his shirt, which is constantly wet. I decided to work with him using Focusing. I invited him to describe the feeling of sucking.

Ronald said, "Like a penis in my mouth and I like that feeling ... it's calm when I suck ... it makes me calm ..."
I asked him how he experiences the reactions of others. He said it disturbs him when someone reacts. He understands that the others find his sucking disgusting, but he can't help himself. Without a finger in his mouth, his mouth feels too large and empty. Then I said:
"Just draw how you are feeling today ..."
Ronald drew yellow figures.
"How does your mouth feel with your finger in it?"
With yellow he drew the boys who abused him.
"How does your mouth feel without a finger in it?"
With red he drew a gigantic mouth.

I noticed that Ronald was beginning to relax. Then, another expression appeared on his face. He said he didn't want to suck any longer, but that he couldn't draw that. Now Ronald carries his drawing with him at all times. If he wants to suck, his hand strokes the drawing. He also uses this at school. His teacher tried to change the behavior by forbidding him to suck. Ronald said this didn't help at all. We agreed on certain times when he wouldn't suck. He does not suck at school, when he talks, or when he is busy with his hands. He goes along with this agreement, especially since he has the drawing. So far, our agreement is working out fairly well. The other children in the group also have a place to draw. Sometimes they draw all over the table as if they can't stop themselves. Afterwards their faces beam as if they have been released. Thanks. Hortance.

Reflection:
After no more than a three-hour introduction, Hortance is able to accompany Ronald on a successful Focusing experience. Now that she has discovered the power of Focusing, she can continue to practice and develop her skill.

Focusing at Suriname was introduced by a workshop, but often this process is introduced by a staff member who has learned the method elsewhere. Introducing something new requires courage, but usually this person's enthusiasm is great and overcomes initial skepticism.

WHERE CAN YOU START?

You start wherever you are currently working. For instance, a child psychologist introduces Focusing to her clients in a children's hospital. She works with chronically ill children as part of a treatment team that includes a pediatrician, a nurse, and a physical therapist. In this example she is working with a thirteen-year-old girl whose verbal expression is limited. Without the invitation to take a journey inside, the process might have gotten stuck.

Judith works with children who are expected to die young. The emphasis of her work is to improve the children's quality of life.

One of Judith's patients is Wanda. As a result of her illness, Wanda is extremely thin. Her bright blue eyes stand out against her pale face. She lives with her mother and grandmother. Her nurse reports that she never expresses her feelings or says anything about what she needs or desires. She never speaks about her condition or how cystic fibrosis affects her life.

Judith's first goal is to develop a rapport with Wanda. Their initial meetings are short and Wanda refuses the invitation to draw or to talk. Judith starts a conversation, shows interest and asks questions, but she notices that this does not stimulate real contact.

One day, she invites Wanda to take a "journey inside," a journey in which her body will be her guide. First, Wanda brings her attention inside. Judith asks what it is like in there and whether she can draw what she notices. Wanda draws two rocks with a blue stream running between them. In the middle of the stream she draws a ring with a sparkly stone. Judith can see in Wanda's eyes that her attention is turned inward. Also Wanda waits as if sensing something. Then she draws herself standing under the sparkly ring. She has rainbow-colored hair and a rainbow skirt.

Wanda tells a story that goes with the drawing. She explains that there is a weakness in her chest. A fairy has lost the ring that holds her magic powers. The ring was swept away by a river. Even if the fairy were to find the ring it would be of no use now because she is weak and unprotected.

The girl relates that she went to look inside herself to see if she could find the fairy's magic power. That was when the girl with the rainbow hair and the magic rainbow skirt appeared. The rainbow feeling gives Wanda strength. She points out that the weak feeling is only inside her chest.

After summer vacation, Wanda returns for treatment. Her contact with the felt sense is more intense, but still with few words. She smiles at Judith with an open, happy expression and says that this drawing is their first collaboration. Now, Wanda can feel a connection to her illness and also to the power she needs to live with it.

Reflection:

By inviting Wanda to focus, Judith sidesteps verbal communication. Not every child has the words to express what is going on inside. Through Focusing, Wanda discovers a resource inside her that enables her not to remain a prisoner of her illness.

INTRODUCING A FOCUSING PROGRAM IN SCHOOL OR OTHER INSTITUTIONS

Perhaps you are that single enthusiastic individual who wishes to be a catalyst for an entire Focusing program. If you wish to launch a program at a school or any other institution, it's a good idea to meet with someone in charge and give them verbal and written information about Focusing. Know that even a description of Focusing can bring up highly personal and sometimes perplexing responses from others. Some adults are fearful about making contact with their bodily experiences. Partly for this reason, it's important to have the leaders of the institution allied with your intention.

Whether you're introducing Focusing to children or adults,

participation should be strictly voluntary. In the context of a school, some teachers may distance themselves from a Focusing program and decline to participate. Often such people are influenced by fear. They may be afraid that they will become too deeply involved with the children's personal lives. Quite rightly, they do not want to be responsible for their students' emotional lives as well as for their academic performance. In practice, this concern rarely arises *after* Focusing has been introduced.

There are other concerns you will want to be address. Some teachers worry that the use of Focusing will result in a loss of discipline in the school. They may fear that they will be required to give up rules that are necessary for order and safety.

A Focusing trainer in Budapest works as one of two teachers in a classroom. Her colleague is very directive and solves conflicts using strict discipline and even threats. For most of the year he seems entirely uninterested in Focusing. However, after nine months of co-teaching, he expresses curiosity about what it is she does with the children. He confesses that he is frightened of losing control of the class. That is why he is so strict. He says he realizes that because he doesn't trust the children, they don't trust him.

It should be clear by now, that Focusing never requires a teacher to give up things that are good. You can use Focusing in a classroom and also maintain order and safety. In fact, you can add Focusing to any other teaching method and it will bring more space and peace to you and the children.

Focusing has been used in tandem with social skills training, getting-along workshops, etc. and the Focusing always improves the results and effectiveness of other skills. Focusing is more about *how* than *what*. When the school counselor learns of these results, he or she wants to add Focusing to the counseling repertoire.

Of course teachers and other professionals need to have the freedom to choose whether or not to participate in a Focusing program. That said, it can be disruptive for children to go from Focusing one year to not Focusing the next year. In school settings, there are a few ways to get around this.

One boy, who is very upset in class, remarks: "Last year I was allowed to draw my feelings when I was very angry and that helped."
The teacher replies: "If you know how to do that, you can do it right now." She gives the child room to draw what he feels inside.

Another teacher who does not yet know Focusing finds a different solution. She asks a teacher in the classroom next to hers whether a boy who is having problems can join her "clearing a space" group.

Another often-heard complaint is that there simply isn't time for yet another special program such as Focusing. The school day is already packed and even a once-a-week, 45-minute commitment can sound like too much. Surprisingly, using the basic Focusing attitude does not require additional time. Many Focusing interventions take just a few minutes. In a one-on-one conversation, you simply ask the three questions, "Where in your body do you notice that? How does it feel there? How does it want to be expressed?" There's a major benefit to these gentle questions: the child feels better and ready to move forward. That might be enough to convert any teacher!

About three months after learning to focus, Bettina from Germany says she experiences far fewer conflicts in the classroom. She finds that she does not have to be authoritarian to maintain order. Indeed, whenever she notices herself becoming rigid, she makes contact with herself inside. Focusing comes to the rescue and says: "Stop. Something wants to be heard here." In this way, she avoids blocking out her feelings. The words have been burned into her: each child wants to be heard. "I know that," she says, "and I do not want to forget it."

How to involve parents

If you're going to launch a Focusing program with children, it is important to inform the parents early on and even give them a taste of what you'll be doing. At the first parent-teacher meeting of the year, connect with parents over the worries and joys of raising children. You can affirm that raising children is not an easy task. Next, bring up the topic of listening. Point out that listening is different from offering insight and advice. It's about making space for what's inside the child and really receiving that.

If you are speaking to parents at a primary school, you can emphasize that Focusing increases children's self-reliance and improves their concentration. It can also help clear emotional blocks that contribute to absenteeism.

Explain to parents the guidelines of the Focusing program. Some of these may differ from what they are used to.

• First, ask the parents to respect their children's privacy. Their children should be permitted or invited — but not required — to talk about their Focusing experiences at the school.

- Invite the parents to contact you if they notice changes at home, good or bad. For your part, promise to reach out to parents if their child has a noteworthy or unusual experience with Focusing. You can explain that in such a situation, you will need to first ask the child's permission.
- Emphasize that the children's Focusing drawings are kept at school.
- Let parents know that while you cannot report exactly what a child is drawing or saying, you can discuss in a general way how the child is doing.

If you have time, lead an exercise with the parents so that they can experience the power of this special type of listening. Firsthand experience is more persuasive than any words you say. It is helpful in the long run for parents to be familiar with the Focusing process. When both the school and the parents take a Focusing approach, each reinforces the other.

At a day-care center, the teachers take time at a parent's night to show them an edited video of a Focusing class. For this group of parents, seeing is believing.

A variation of the following letter may be used to inform parents about a new Focusing program:

Starting in October, I will be working with the day-care groups at Het Telraam one morning every two weeks. I will also be coaching the caretakers so that they can expand their professional repertoire. I would like to introduce myself to you and show you how I work with babies, toddlers and preschoolers and how I coach caregivers to do the same. In the next few weeks I will be contacting you to schedule a meeting.

The principle that underlies all my work with babies, toddlers and preschoolers is that they are very wise inside. I seek to connect to that wisdom. If we listen well and with respect, we can help them find their own solutions. Also, by listening carefully we help young children find their limits and respect adults' limits. Children understand so much if we are able to speak from their perspective.

As a child therapist I have developed a speciality in observing, listening to and talking to babies, toddlers and preschoolers. It turns out that listening and carefully verbalizing their inner felt experiences helps children with both minor and major troubles. These are the troubles that manifest themselves in frequent crying and sleeplessness.

One key to this process is that by watching the small person's non-verbal behavior we can check to see whether our response has been correct. That is, we can check to see whether we have struck the right note and matched the child's inner feeling. If we have, then the child's behavior can change.

There are so many pleasant, exciting, and frightening experiences in young children's lives. They can only understand these in their own way. Their experiences may include encountering strange faces, going on a visit, the incubator, being admitted to a hospital, facing a longer-than-usual absence of Mom or Dad. These experiences can be tolerated — they can even be sources of growth — if we listen to the child from the inside out and offer the words that fit the feeling inside.

At the day-care center I will have short conversations with the babies and toddlers and I will train the caretakers there to do so as well. I will videotape my conversations so that they can be used as teaching tools. All of this is subject to your approval. I hope you will agree to let your child participate. And I hope I will have the opportunity to meet you very soon.

How Focusing relates to psychotherapy

Many teachers and administrators wonder about the relationship of Focusing to psychotherapy. They wonder what to do when something serious comes up. How do you know when Focusing is not enough? When do you recommend a child for further counseling? Different situations require different solutions.

Alice is a highly intelligent little girl in Miss Katline's class. Her performance is strong in every subject. She is a true perfectionist. However it is difficult for Alice to connect with the other kids in her class. She expresses frustration, even despair, about how hard it is to make friends. Her parents maintain, when approached by Miss Katline, that everything will turn out fine.

One morning Miss Katline finds Alice angry and in tears. "Nobody wants to play with me," she cries, "they all think I'm stupid". Miss Katline takes her to a quiet spot. As best she can, she names Alice's feelings, emphasizing the ones that are clearly visible. Alice expresses a lot of emotion about the things she dreads. She says: "Everything is so difficult, it's like having to climb an incredibly high mountain."

Miss Katline asks whether Alice would like to draw that mountain on a piece of paper. Alice draws a mountain full of problems; the paths are snarled by all the situations that block her way in life. Miss Katline asks whether the drawing has something more to say. Alice smiles and says she doesn't want to draw anymore. She wants to go to her classroom and get back to work.

Miss Katline is left with some questions: "Can I just do that? Isn't that crossing a boundary? Aren't I taking on the role of a psychotherapist?" As she connects to her felt sense she notices that, from inside, the answer to these last two questions is "no." Alice went back to the classroom a very relieved girl, and Miss Katline can sense the good in that. She decides to schedule a meeting with Alice's parents. After some conversation they acknowledge that being highly intelligent can create some problems for Alice. The parents learn that they can help Alice by listening to her attentively.

Focusing with children can bring up difficult feelings that may take a teacher (or parent) by surprise. Some problems may be beyond your ability to help. If such a problem arises, acknowledge your limits. Consider a consultation or referral to another professional. In some situations a therapist's guidance is necessary because the child needs more than simply the teacher listening to what's inside.

A Focusing trainer in Canada leads her class in clearing a space. She reads from a prepared text: "Hello, nice child ... Maybe you have a problem or something difficult ... something that you experienced ... today ... yesterday ... a long time ago ... or something that's going to happen tomorrow ... something that is bothering you now."

One girl makes a drawing and writes in large letters: "Help! What now?" From her drawing, the teacher understands that the child is facing a serious problem. She consults the girl and then gets in touch with school management. After conversation with the parents, a team of professionals is called in.

Without clearing a space. this little girl's pain might not have been heard, and she and her family might not have received the needed help.

When a serious matter comes up, the question of whether or not to involve the parents deserves particular attention. If it is possible, it is best to involve them. Your first step, however, is to take time for the child. Try to get an understanding of the situation as the child puts it into words. It can be hard to get the concrete information you need from a drawing. The best thing to do is to sit down with the child in private and ask whether the drawing has something to say. Pay particular attention to the "something" inside that does not want to speak or is afraid to speak.

After talking with the child, you may confer with a supervisor, so that you do not have to bear the burden of the information alone. Do not do this, however, without the child's knowledge. To do so would damage the bond of trust between you. The child might be tempted to conclude: "They never take me seriously. They just do whatever they want with me." Listen to what the child has to say and explain very firmly that the problem cannot continue as it is. Remain firm about the necessity of involving other adults. You might say something like:

> You have behaved as best you could. Can you leave it to the adults to find the best way out? This situation is very bad for you, and we can't let it go on like this.

FOCUSING IN FAMILY THERAPY

> Laura, a Focusing trainer in Budapest, uses Focusing skills when she counsels a small group of divorced mothers with children between the ages of five and ten. The aim of the counseling is to help the mothers and children integrate the experience of divorce so that it does not obstruct healthy development. She finds that Focusing can engage the child and the adult equally well.
>
> Laura and her clients meet weekly for two-hour sessions. They start by letting their attention go inside and asking: "What does it look like in there today? Is anything asking for special attention?" During some sessions they select a certain subject to focus on. Laura accompanies them as they turn their attention inward and they draw whatever that certain subject brings up. Often this creates space for some new element of the bodily experience to be expressed. After this new element is heard, the outward behavior has room to change.
>
> Through their drawings, the mothers and children tell their inner stories. During the discussion that follows, everyone listens attentively. Surprising feelings and experiences are shared. In the end, the family members understand each other better and feel a greater sense of tolerance and solidarity.

Laura's caring, empathic attention provides the safety for everyone in the group to find the space to develop.

12

Especially for Parents

A mother called me on the phone and asked me for advice on what to do with her boys age three and four. First I told her to take a course on Focusing with children. Then I told her to ask her son, as soon as he complained of a bad feeling, to see if he could find where he felt it in his body and how it felt there. After that he could imagine putting it somewhere outside of himself, so he could have a better look at it. Some weeks later she told me the following story:

> *I was driving the car with my two sons in the back. The youngest one was angry, crying and shouting and I was upset. I couldn't get a clear idea what was going on and I needed to concentrate on driving the car.*
>
> *Joachim, the elder boy, asked Casimir, the little one*: Where do you feel the anger inside?
>
> *Casimir responded between his heavy sobs*: In my stomach,
>
> *Joachim*: Where exactly do you feel it?
>
> *Casimir*:   Here, *and he put his little hand on his stomach.*
>
> *Joachim*: Keep your hand there for a while because then you can feel it better.
>
> *Casimir*:   Not nice there.
>
> *Joachim*: Now put it outside … you give it a place somewhere … you let it go … and you will be happy again.
>
> *Then it became very quiet in the back of the car, the boys were content and I felt very relieved.*

I have started with this example to emphasize that Focusing by children is not difficult. Even an instruction by telephone can have consequences. And even children can learn it. (This example is taken from the article *Children Focusing: Guiding and Teaching Children to Focus* by Marta Stapert, available from <www.focusing.org/chfc/article_index.html>.)

ALL AGES

Does it happen in your family that you don't pay much attention to your child until you intervene, adjust and give direction? At all ages you can improve your relationship with your children by giving them attention, not only when you are intervening in some difficulty, but at other times as well. Here a father has the right idea, although it does not turn out as planned.

> *It is the first time this month that Gerda's father manages to be home before seven o'clock. He finishes work two hours earlier than usual in order to be home with Gerda tonight. He picks up his daughter from school and intends not to read the newspaper and not to watch television, but just pay attention to her. Once they are at home Gerda starts playing with her dolls. She is so engrossed in her game that she doesn't have eyes or ears for her father. Father is facing a dilemma: does he let her do her own thing and play without him interfering? Or should he step in and play with his child? In the end, Father gives Gerda the opportunity to play alone but he remains attentive and near her, without reading a newspaper, and without watching television.*

Reflection:
> *You notice that Gerda's father gives her space. How would Gerda feel if her father obliged her to play with him? The father just remains present and if Gerda wants him to play with her, then he is available to do so.*

Contrast this father with the efforts of another father who has learned accepting language, but who receives an unexpected reaction.

> *This morning Ellen wants to say something to her father. After breakfast she starts to talk about what happened at school the day before. Every so often her father looks at her and nods, even makes a comment. He also checks his watch several times; he has a personnel meeting this morning that he can't afford to miss. Ellen notices that her father is distracted and stops her story in the middle of a sentence.*

In many failed encounters, the non-verbal message says, "it's not possible now" or "I don't have time for this" and brushes the communication aside. You reveal something about yourself and about how you view the other person, more by how you say it than what you say.

Whether you give your full attention or not, your overall attitude will be evident to your children. Your attitude is in everything. (See Chapter 9, *The Focusing Attitude*.) For instance, when talking, you pass on an implicit message through the intonation of your voice. Here is a game to play with your children. How many ways are there to ask a single question, such as: *"Would you like a cup of tea?"*

You can take on different attitudes and facial expressions when you ask the question. You can vary the tone of your voice. The question remains the same: *"Would you like a cup of tea?"* The only thing that changes is the way in which you ask, from neutral to irritated, from persuasive to forceful.

It is important to be aware of the difference between *what* is taking place and *how* it is taking place. *What* is asked has much less influence on the communication than *how* it is asked. The child has radar for this. For example, she might think, *"It sounds as if she is in a hurry so I'd better say 'no,' although it sounded nice to me."*

Your attitude is also evident in how you word your requests. Here is another experiment. As you read the following examples, try to imagine yourself in the child's shoes. Can you feel when the child loses out in this example? When the father loses out? And when there a satisfactory solution for both father and daughter, where both win and both feel satisfied?

> *Because his wife is at work, Father cannot leave his nine-year-old daughter Lisa at home alone. But Lisa is in the middle of an exciting video-game. Father might handle the situation in three different ways.*

The Authoritarian Solution
Father: Lisa, we have to go shopping now.
Lisa: I don't want to go. I'm playing my game.
Father: You know I can't leave you here alone. You're too young. Turn your game off right now.
Lisa: No! Why do I always have to do what you want?
Father: You're such a nuisance. You need to do what I tell you.
How would this dialogue make you feel if you were a child?

The Indulgent Response
Father: Lisa, we should really go shopping.
Lisa: I don't want to go. I'm playing my game.
Father: You never want to go shopping with me.
Lisa: Why don't you just go alone?
Father: You know I can't let you stay home alone. You're too young. [Pause] Fine. Then I'll stay home. You always have

it your own way.

Check once again to see what felt sense this dialogue might create inside of the daughter.

The Empathic Response

Father: I haven't done any shopping for dinner yet. We need to go to the store.

Lisa: I don't want to go. I'm playing my game.

Father: I know it doesn't feel good to interrupt that, but I don't feel comfortable leaving you home alone. You're too young. How long will it be before you finish this level?

Lisa: Just a little while.

Father: OK. I'll wait another few minutes.

Lisa: It's OK if we go now. I can save it and continue playing later.

Reflection:

• *Can you notice in the last example how a turning point occurs? Both father and daughter are satisfied when the right chord is touched. That is what happens when a child feels heard and the adult feels understood. A true conversation begins, and both parties are able to find a good solution.*

• *Can you remember some of your own experiences? Which attitude did your mother or father adopt with you?*

• *What do you see around you on the street and in the supermarket? Have you encountered both authoritarian and indulgent behavior? Do you think the parents are afraid of something? What is each parent afraid of?*

• *As a child, how would you like to be approached? What exactly would enable you to feel understood?*

In general, your attitude can be one of trusting your child's inner wisdom. Even small children possess it, if they are allowed to sense it. The following example shows how a little girl age eighteen months knows where to go and when.

It is granddad's birthday and little Nadia is visiting him with her father, mother and older sister. Her parents tell her beforehand who else will be there: grandma, uncles, aunts and cousins. When they enter the room, Nadia first remains in her mother's arms. She does not want to be put on the ground. Then Nadia notices her favorite uncle. She knows that uncle very well, because he has looked after her. Nadia lets go of her mother and clambers onto her uncle's lap. From there she quietly views

*the bustle around her. A few minutes later she sees her cousin
Cloë playing with building blocks. She gets off his lap and toddles
over to Cloë.*

Reflection:
*You notice that Nadia determines her own pace. Her mother
does not push her into a room full of people. Nadia first uses
the safety of her uncle to make the transition to independent
discovery.*

BABIES

Parents communicate with unborn babies by stroking the pregnant
belly, talking, and even wearing a bell. Early on, the baby learns to
recognize the sound of its parents' voices. After birth, parents and
children are able to connect physically in new ways. The baby can
lie on its parents' bellies or be held close during daily tasks. Some
parents learn infant massage. All of this contributes to the baby's
attachment to its parents.

Focusing can deepen this attachment. Somewhere inside, the
baby knows how it feels. Since babies experience the world in a
global way, they do not distinguish between thoughts, feelings, and
physical sensations. But they do react from their experiences. If
babies feel heard and understood, they will feel safer and more at
peace.

All over the world, parents are Focusing with babies. They notice
with amazement that their babies nurse more easily, fall asleep with
less trouble, and stop crying sooner. As a new parent, you can help
your baby process the experience of being born.

*Dora and her husband adopted a baby. István was four weeks
old when they first saw him and six weeks old when they were
allowed to take him home. In the hospital Dora talks to István
about his history. In detail, she puts his experiences into words.*

Dora explains: "Bit by bit I told him everything I could imagine
about how he was born ... how he suddenly missed his
mother ... what it must have felt like for him inside the
womb ... how strange the world must have seemed to him
when he was born ... how awful I thought that must have
been for him. I described how we chose him and no one
else ... how strange I must have smelled to him ... how
even my voice must have sounded unusual. I described how
happy we were to take him home ... to his home forever ...

and that he would see his little kittycat that was already
waiting for him. I loved talking to him like that, it made me
feel very connected to him. Each time I spoke he looked at
me attentively as if he understood exactly what I was
saying."

Reflection:
   • *Can you sense how these intimate talks between mother
   and baby would strengthen the attachment between them?*
   • *Despite the major changes he has experienced, István comes
   across as a calm, contented baby. Could this be related to the
   empathic mirroring Dora offers?*

ELEMENTARY SCHOOL YEARS

During the elementary school years you want to do and experience
things together with your child. You can empathize without getting
over-concerned. If children share their emotions with their parents,
and parents share their emotions with their children, a solid foundation
comes into being for the family. It goes without saying that *when*
parents do share emotions with children — something that doesn't
happen often enough — this should be adapted to the emotional
level of the child.

   Besides doing things together, there should also be recognition
of the contribution each member makes to the family. Often parents,
with these contributions in mind, formulate questions that start "Would
you like to ...?"
   "Would you mind setting the table please?"
   "Do you want to come and sit at the table for dinner?"
   "Would you please clear away your shoes?"

An adult hears those questions differently from children. An adult
hears that you want them to do something. Children think you are
asking them whether they want to do it or not and they need time to
think about it, in order to give an answer. As a parent it is better to
assume that there are certain tasks for them to do because it is *a
habit* in your family to take care of some things together.
   It follows that it is not always necessary to ask them if they
want to do something. You need only *remind* them of what has been
agreed upon beforehand.
   What if your child doesn't do what he is told? Do you scream
and scold? You wouldn't scream at an adult if he forgot to do the
dishes. What if you first asked your child for information and then
reminded her of your agreement?

"I see that the dishes are still in the sink. I need that space cleared. It is your job. How come the dishes haven't been done yet? I can give you five minutes."

Consider how many times a child hears "no" or "don't" in his life: "Don't touch the books," "Don't put your feet on the sofa," "Don't leave your school bag in the hallway," "Don't speak with your mouth full," "Don't bully." The adult's dissatisfaction causes the child to feel powerless.

Children set high standards for themselves. They want so much to do well. Many children are plagued by a fear of failure. Over time, such children can develop a critical voice inside that can stop them at every turn. The voice says things like, "I am stupid," "I never do anything right," "No matter what I do, they don't love me."

Does this voice sound familiar? Can you imagine the kind of impact it could have on a child? It is extremely difficult for parents to resist the urge to push their children toward greater achievement and success and even more difficult to communicate to them that what matters is who they are, not what they achieve. Can you imagine letting a child sense that he is fine just the way he is? If you can, you'll go a long way toward boosting the child's resilience and, in turn, his performance.

Of course it is important to continue to set limits, but the way you do this can be guided by the basic Focusing attitude. For example, if your daughter throws her school bag in the hallway every evening after school, you might want to correct this behavior. What would it be like for your daughter to hear you say: "You've just come home from school and you've had a long day. Now your bag is in the hallway. Will you take it upstairs with you in a minute or two?"

Do you notice the mirroring in these sentences?

One mother took this a step further. Every day for several days she said: "Shall I take your bag upstairs with me? I don't mind doing it because I know you've had a hard day." After a few days of this, her daughter took the bag upstairs of her own accord!

When the critical voice inside becomes excessively negative, Focusing can provide a solution. Through learning to listen to her true self, the child can liberate herself from exaggerated self-criticism. She learns to accept herself as a person with both limitations and potentials. This acceptance allows change to occur far sooner than it otherwise would.

ADOLESCENCE

Much parenting is about watching your children grow towards

independence. You soon realize that you can't protect your child everywhere. Your presence functions like a point of contact in difficult moments, and will continue to do so even when your children are grown.

The growth towards independence is continuous but it has peaks, especially during adolescence. This time is one of detachment from parents, often accompanied by fear. Fiercely opposing the parental rules, joining active movements whose values are far removed from the parents' values, the young person is rattling the door to the parents' soul.

The adolescent is in search of his own identity, just like the two-year-old toddler who says "I won't!" but the obvious "I am who I am" is gone and the adolescent goes in search of his own self. In fact, his whole notion of self is questioned during the major social, cognitive and physical changes of adolescence.

This extrication from the family is marked by the importance that "others" acquire for the adolescent. The objective is to achieve autonomy in both tasks and emotions. This objective is aided by the relationships that the adolescent develops with other people.

During this time, you, as a parent, need to keep sufficient distance. The adolescent needs the opportunity to develop independently. This does not mean that your parenting disappears. You remain available when it is necessary. The adolescent experiences that you are there, but that you do not push yourself into his process.

> *One mother reports: I have a lot of trouble with my sixteen-year-old daughter, who refuses to help out around the house. She lives in our house like a stranger and it just infuriates me. I really value collaboration.*
>
> *Since learning Focusing, I approach my interactions with her differently. I listen to her carefully and repeat what she says, without adding comments, advice, or questions. I am finding it more and more fun. It actually gives me a feeling of freedom.*
>
> *And, for the first time in a long while, we had a personal talk. She told me that everyone finds her tough and independent, but that inside she feels insecure and weak. She asked me about Focusing and whether I thought it could help her. I told her that Focusing is about finding out how it feels inside the body. I gave her something to read. I kept myself at a distance, spoke laconically, not too eagerly, and I feel good about that.*

By taking a step back this mother gave her daughter the chance to step forward.

Once children are older than twenty, it is the author's experience that it is not hard to focus with them again. Even now my grown children ask me to listen to them as they work out difficult issues. They know when they want to discuss content and when they don't want to reveal content and they know that I respect this. Unbeknownst to me, one of my sons recently programmed my computer to display a screensaver that reads: "Have you focused today?"

FOCUSING PROVIDES EMOTIONAL SUPPORT

Focusing provides a way to give emotional support to children of all ages when they need it. Parents often don't understand why their child is upset. The child lacks the means to explain, or the child doesn't understand herself. Maybe she's afraid her parents will judge instead of listen. Focusing gives parents the tools both to support and to understand their child.

> *Mother is picking seven-year-old Anke up after a birthday party. Anke is terribly angry. She clenches her hands into fists; her eyes fixate on her mother. "I want to get away from here."*
> *To Anke it is clear why she is angry: at Sien's party she felt as if the others were laughing at her. Sien and her friend kept laughing every time Anke looked at them. Mother wants to find out what really happened.*

Reflection:
> • *Everything that is happening within is not clear to Anke initially. There is a feeling of anger and a feeling that that she does not belong, that she is less worthy compared to Sien because Sien has her own pony ... and maybe something more.*
> • *She wants to express her inner knowing.*
> • *Anke's mother listens. By reflecting Anke's words without judgment, Anke's mother helps her daughter dig up more about her feelings. This gives the girl a feeling of relief. The mother gets a different view of the situation and also finds she can give support simply by listening.*

Sometimes children are inclined to keep painful experiences hidden. Usually this situation is distressing to parents and they try to find out what the problem is.

"Why are you always annoyed by the other children?"

"It's OK to tell me what's going on ... "

"Why don't you sit in your chair for a little while?"

In response to such questions a child may look at his mother or father without uttering a single word or perhaps storm off with an angry outburst. This kind of reaction can leave a parent feeling truly powerless.

Parents should try to answer some 'why' questions themselves:
Why do you get so angry when your child leaves a mess?
Why do you talk so much?
Why are you just sitting around?
Why are you so quick to get offended?

These questions are difficult to answer. "Why" questions in general put a person on the defensive.

Some parents notice that their children make the same type of excuses again and again, always blaming something or someone. It's as though the child believes nothing can be changed. He does not experience anything new and no change occurs in his behavior.

Focusing can bring helpful direction to problem solving. It can also change the relationship between parents and children. When parents and children focus together, a special bond develops.

Usually one parent is the first to learn about Focusing and its helpfulness in exploring personal issues. This parent may introduce Focusing to the children. Often the other parent hangs back, taking a "wait and see" approach. As long as the second parent is basically supportive, the Focusing attitude can permeate family life, bringing greater understanding, closeness, and respect. But if there is conflict between parents about the use of Focusing, children may sense this and pull away from the process.

When you start out, you may make the mistake of repelling children with your enthusiasm, or you might try to use the process to manipulate a situation to your advantage.

> *Taking a course on "Focusing with children," a mother has just begun to introduce the process to her twelve-year-old son. In the middle of an argument she suddenly asks: "And how does it feel inside when you are fighting me like this?" Her son shouts back: "You stick to focusing yourself and keep me out of it!" She reacts: "You are right, this is not the right moment to ask you something like that. I moved too quickly."*

Without fail, a child will sense if you are using Focusing in an inappropriate way. The Focusing attitude requires the greatest possible honesty.

When you adopt the Focusing attitude and make it part of your communication in your family, it can help with all sorts of problems.

Sandra is the mother of two boys, ages 6 and 8. She uses Focusing in her personal life, on the job, and with her children when the occasion arises. Her children are familiar with Focusing and have a sense of what to do when she invites them to listen inside.

Sandra has taken her sons to see a play. In it, one of the characters fights a seven-headed dragon and the dragon roars loudly. Later that evening Sandra's son, André, calls to her from his bedroom. She notices that he is upset, but she also wants to maintain the family rule that children do not get out of bed after bedtime.

André: I keep hearing that dragon in my head and now I can't sleep.

Mother sits on his bed and he crawls onto her lap.

Sandra: Such a noise that dragon is making in your head ... Shall we do something about it?

André: Yes.

Sandra: Shall we sit with it in a friendly way ... with all that scariness that you feel in your head?

André: Yes.

Sandra: Can you point out where you feel that scariness the most?

André: Here in my head and nowhere else.

André points to his temples.

André: It is pressing there ... I don't want to sit with it ... it has to go.

Sandra: Do you want to put that dragon some place else?

André: Yes, I am throwing it very far away.

With both hands André makes a big throwing gesture.

Sandra: How is it now in your head? Does it feel different?

André: No, it is still there.

Sandra: It's good to just sit with it ... Maybe you want to put it into something that has a lid ... a pot or a box or something like that ...

André: Yes. In a box with a cover.

André sighs with relief and crawls back under the covers.

Sandra: Nice, isn't it, that you can do something about it when something is bothering you inside ...

André: (very softly) Yes.

Reflection:

André is used to Focusing with his mother's invitations as prompts. In less than two minutes he has made enough space

*for himself that he can sleep. There is no irritation or conflict
between Sandra and André. Sandra is able to maintain a family
rule, and André's fear is heard.*

THE FOCUSING ATTITUDE PREVENTS SERIOUS PROBLEMS

Even with their parents' abundant love and support, children are
bound to struggle with losses, changes and disruptions. In every
child's life, some difficult events will take place. The child may switch
to another class or get a new teacher. His friend moves away, or he
himself moves to a new home. The child may be in an accident or be
hospitalized. A new brother or sister may be born. A grandmother or
grandfather may die. The child may witness his parents fighting and
wonder if his parents are going to get divorced.

There is also the outside world. The child may witness an accident
or other upsetting event. He learns about natural and man-made
disasters: floods, earthquakes and wars. He may find that in some
places children are starving or mistreated.

Children can handle a lot. They are highly inventive and can
draw upon their inner strength in hard times. Sometimes, though,
difficult experiences come at the expense of their development. When
children are bothered by something, they are prevented from using
their full capacities.

There is a preventive effect when you help a child pay attention
to what's inside. Negative experiences are less likely to accumulate
and block the child's progress. You do not have to focus with your
child in order to achieve this. The basic Focusing attitude can be
enough. In time you'll develop a nose for what needs more attention.
Remain alert to what your child is expressing. Sometimes a child
appears to be handling something comfortably, but inside this is not
the case.

*Machteld is thirteen and on vacation with her family. While she
is playing with friends in the swimming pool, a boy dives into
the water and lands on top of her. She is completely submerged
and comes up spluttering. At the edge of the swimming pool
she loses consciousness for a short time.*

*Machteld's father, a doctor, attends to her very carefully.
He can see that medically there is nothing wrong. A little while
later Machteld gets back into the pool. It seems to her father
that she wants to put on a brave face for her peers.*

*After dinner Machteld's father comes and sits next to her.
He asks if it is all right to give some friendly attention to what
happened in the pool. At first Machteld does not want to. She*

tells her father that the incident has been forgotten. But her father senses that inside, something is distressed. Machteld agrees to spend a little time with her feelings. She is familiar with Focusing. She takes out paper and crayons. Her father simply remains present and mirrors her words.

Once Machteld is connected to what's inside, she draws a yellow background. Yellow is her safe color. Then shades of blue come, first light and then darker, stronger lines. Her hands shoot out in powerful strokes. Red and black are added. One part of the page remains conspicuously empty. Machteld carefully avoids it.

Machteld: It is so terribly angry inside. I couldn't handle how angry I was. I was so angry that I stopped breathing. I just felt myself sink. I couldn't stay with it any longer. Now I see it come back again ... It's as if there is a bridge hanging. I can see colors there again.

She fills the empty part of the page with light colors. Her face becomes relaxed and she sighs deeply.

Machteld: Now I feel everything inside again. Tomorrow I'm going to tell him that he shouldn't do something stupid like that ever again.

Reflection:

• *Do you notice how important it is for Machteld to deal with her anger? The anger is linked to her fainting. By providing an opportunity for Machteld to hear her anger, her father has prevented it from accumulating inside. Now Machteld knows that she doesn't have to repress her anger.*

• *Through symbolizing, the blank inside Machteld gets filled up again. She is able to make a bridge to her actions when she was very angry.*

13

How Adults Focus

This chapter outlines the Focusing process for adults. Focusing can be defined as paying attention to a bodily sense of some aspect of your experience, which is often felt only vaguely at first but can also be a strong, overwhelming sensation. By sitting patiently and respectfully with what you are feeling inside, you can learn what your *felt sense* has to say. This inner "something" begins to move, and brings about change in small steps.

Remember that is this process the body knows which direction to take. If you follow the sentences below, you can experience this for yourself.

> *Take the time to let your attention go inside.*
> *Do you know the feeling you have in your body when something is done ... when you've taken care of something you needed to do?*
> *Do you remember the relief you felt when you made it somewhere just in time?*
> *In these moments something reacts inside. You can feel it clearly. It's as though something shifts or expands, becoming lighter.*
> *Take a moment to recall what it's like to find something you thought you lost. Or the feeling of discovering that something difficult in your life will be resolved.*
> *Do you notice a shift?*

This is called the *felt shift*. It is a physically experienced change. With this shift you feel a sense of rightness and an easement in the body.

OUTLINE OF THE STEPS

In order to teach Focusing to others, Dr. Eugene Gendlin initially divided the process into six steps. In actual fact, each time you use the process, it will be unique. Sometimes you'll move through a step quickly; other times a certain step will demand a lot of attention. Not all the steps will be followed every time. These steps form the basic structure, but it is a very flexible structure.

Four steps form the core of the Focusing process. They are: *discovering a felt sense, finding a handle, resonating,* and *receiving.* Two more steps, *asking and exploring* and *clearing a space,* allow you to deepen the process. They also help move things along when you get stuck.

Of course, as a pre-step, you need to let your attention go inside. An outline of the Focusing process might look like this:

- Letting your attention go inside
- The core steps
  Discovering a felt sense
  Finding a handle
  Resonating
  Receiving
- Further steps that support the process
  Asking/exploring
  Clearing a space

Letting your attention go inside
Letting your attention go inside requires some preparation. If you are going to pay attention to your inner experience, you need to make a time and space for it. Choose a place where you feel safe and comfortable. No special posture is necessary. Let your body know it will be there for a while. You may want to close your eyes.

There are different ways of letting the attention go inside. If you can already do it, feel free to use your own method. Note, however, that in Focusing, attention does not remain in the mind, as in a strictly thinking process. Neither does it go as deep as in a meditative process. It remains somewhere in between.

You can use the following text to guide your attention inward:

Feel your feet making contact with the floor ...
Feel how your body makes contact with the chair, the back of the chair and the seat ...
Feel how your head is connected to your torso ...
Listen to your breathing without changing anything about it ...
Feel the movement of your breath ...
With every exhalation, allow your attention to travel deeper inside ...
Let your attention sink down to the middle area of your body, the place where you feel your own depth ...
Be sure to be aware of the torso, chest and stomach area ...
Once you have arrived there, create an atmosphere that is warm

and mild, open and receptive to anything that may come ...

Take the time now to read through this text once more. Stop after each sentence and either close your eyes or find something neutral to look at. Don't proceed to the next sentence until you feel in your body that a connection has been made.

The core steps
Read the paragraphs below and digest the sentences in italics one by one. Take time with this experience. Trust your body. Allow yourself to wait and see what comes.

Discovering your felt sense

Once you have turned your attention inward, ask yourself: *What wants my attention now?* Wait respectfully and see what comes. Allow your body, not your mind, to answer the question. It can be amazing to realize that the body knows what needs to be heard. It might be a problem, a question you're wondering about, or an event you are anticipating. The situations that occupy your mind are linked to the body.

> *Keeping your attention inside yourself, take time to imagine the situation you want to focus on. Really imagine yourself in this situation. Notice when you begin to feel something in your body.*
> *Usually the felt sense comes up in the part of your body where you breathe — somewhere between your throat and your pelvis. Be friendly and patient even if it is vague or unclear.*
> *Stay with it, giving it your attention. Allow it to unfold in its own way.*
> *Ask yourself if there is a word to describe how it feels. Is it itchy ... chilly ... like an iron bar ... like a fist ... like a chick ... like a balloon? Searching for this word will deepen your connection to the felt sense. No matter what comes, take it seriously ... even when nothing comes.*

Staying in touch with a felt sense is the essence of Focusing. If you lose contact, go back to it. Stay with the felt sense until you notice even a small change inside.

Finding a handle

Let the felt sense tell you how it wants to be described. Don't force it. Let the symbolizing of it — a word, gesture, sound, or image— come from the felt sense itself. When you find one of these symbols that matches the felt sense, you'll notice a feeling of relief and a shift inside. Now the often surprising moment occurs, when something new comes out.

> *Wait until a word ... image ... movement ... color ... or smell emerges ...*
> *Take time here, remaining open to everything that comes.*
> *If you notice something, stay with it ... say hello to it ... give it some friendly attention, even if it is fear or another difficult physical sensation.*
> *Allow what's inside to begin its own story.*
> *Check and see how this "something" inside responds to your attention.*

By saying "hello" to something, you accept that it is the way it is for the moment. This is a precious moment in the process. It is the start of communication with your inner experience. Sometimes you may not like what you encounter inside. Even then, take a patient attitude and give it a greeting in recognition. Allow your body to tell you want it wants you to know.

Resonating

Resonating is the process of checking whether the handle — the word, the image, or other symbol of the felt sense — matches what you feel inside your body. If it does match, it will be like a handle, allowing you to "catch hold" of the felt sense and maintain it in your awareness. This is a step you can apply again and again. Whenever you find a way of expressing or symbolizing the felt sense, check it against what you feel inside.

> *Do these words fit with what you are experiencing?*
> *Go back and forth with your attention, moving between the felt sense and the word, image, or gesture that has come to describe it.*
> *If the description fits, your body will confirm it. When you get a feeling of agreement, when the symbol fits your inner experience exactly, you will feel this in your body. You'll notice that your breathing deepens. Or you may feel a slight tremor. You'll feel as though something has been freed up. Stay with that.*

Sometimes your body lets you know that the handle is right, but that there is something more to be expressed. For example, if the word "suffocating" were to come up, you would ask yourself whether "suffocating" captured your felt sense in its entirety. You might find that another word seems to belong with it. Maybe there's "sadness" there as well. Once again, you ask the felt sense whether "suffocating" and "sad" capture the whole of it. Maybe now your body lets you know that the word "suffocating" still isn't quite right. Then the word "stranglehold" comes up and your whole body suddenly says: "Yes, that is it. 'Like a stranglehold'. That fits much better than 'suffocating'. " By resonating the word with the felt sense, you test it out. Maybe a word like 'restless' comes even closer to your inner experience. Again you test that out, offering it to the felt sense. If you feel any change inside, stay with it.

In summary, resonating is the continuous interaction between your inner experience and the symbol that has come up for it.

Receiving

Throughout the Focusing process, there are moments when something new comes. These may be big steps or small changes. It furthers the process if you welcome each step, however small. This is what we mean by receiving.

When it is time to end, spend a few minutes doing this.

> *Ask inside whether now would be a good moment to end. Check inside whether it has had enough or whether you should focus on this topic again some time in the future.*

It's important to receive and confirm what came, especially anything new, to let it take root. Your problem may not be completely solved, but go ahead and recognize the steps you did take. Recognize that you now know where the issue lives in your body and that you know where to meet up with it again. A step has been made and there will be more steps in the future.

There are a few different ways to end a Focusing process. It depends in part on what your body needs in that moment.

> *Ask your inner self if now would be a good time to end.*
> *Take the time to review your Focusing process, recalling where you started, paying particular attention to anything that was new.*
> *How does it feel in your body now?*
> *Anchor that new feeling in the body so that you can hold on to it ...*
> *Maybe there's something that you want to get back to later ... Maybe there's a spot where you can keep this feeling so you can return to it when the time is right.*

If you want to, end with a thank you. Thank your body for what you've been given. Let it know that you're grateful for it.

Two further steps

In addition to these core steps are another two that Dr. Gendlin describes. These are: *asking/exploring* and *clearing a space.*

Asking/exploring

Sometimes you find a very stable handle and no further meaning emerges. It can be enough that you have found a word that is a good representation of your inner experience. Just naming it can bring a sense of relief. If "stranglehold" was your handle and you resonated with it and it remained "stranglehold," that would mean that your body was satisfied with this name. Still, you might want to discover more about the felt sense that "stranglehold" represents. Asking a question of that inside place can be helpful when your progress seems to stall. Asking questions helps you explore the process.

Asking and exploring take time. In other areas of our lives, the emphasis is to find an answer as quickly as possible. In Focusing, the emphasis is on patience and respect. Answers come only when you listen patiently, with your attention focused on what's inside. Having found a word or image that matches the felt sense, you are going to communicate with your inner self, by using questions to move things along.

The starting point for asking a question is *not knowing*. You are open to new discoveries, ready to be amazed and appreciative of any "answer" that comes. Your attitude toward your inner experience is one of respect and friendliness. Remember, this is not like posing a question to your mind; the mind and the body know different things and answer questions in different ways.

The questions below can be used to further your inner communication. You needn't ask all of them. Just choose those that might clarify your inner process. Note that these are process questions. Content questions, which ask what happened and where and why, are part of the thinking process, while process questions, which explore the "how" of a situation, are better suited for Focusing. They carry your internal journey forward.

What is so "sad"? (Insert your handle here in place of "sad.")
Your objective is to link your inner experience to specific situations in your life. What situation in your life makes this "sadness" come up?

What is this all about?
Again, you are searching for a connection between the "sad" feeling

(or whatever your handle is) and the rest of your life. What is this "sadness" connected to? Does it relate to something in the past? In the present? In the future?

What is the worst thing about this feeling?
Sometimes it's obvious how a felt sense connects to your life. But you don't know what to do about it. Asking "what is the worst of it?" can get at your unique experience.

Is there an emotion here?
Very often there is an emotional quality to an inner experience. It can be useful to explore this.

Is this feeling familiar?
Is this inner experience something you've known before? How long has this been going on? Does it connect in any way to your childhood? Wait for what comes.

Does it need anything? If so, what does it need?
Difficult feelings get stuck inside if they are not heard and given attention. By asking this question you begin to give a felt sense what it needs, even if only in your imagination. Then that emptiness can begin to be filled.

These questions are intended to support your communication with the felt sense. Again, do not answer these questions with your quick-working mind. Wait until your felt sense opens up and offers its own answer. As you communicate with your inner experience, a shift may occur, when you notice that something in your body actually changes. You may feel relief or sigh deeply. These are signs that your inside self has been able to express itself.

Take about thirty minutes right now. *Reread the sentences in italics for the four core steps on pp.141–144, starting with "keeping your attention inside yourself." Pause and see if there's a difficult situation in your life that wants your attention. It is also worthwhile to note the moments when a positive, pleasant feeling comes up. Stay with nice feelings so that they are validated too. Keep reading and checking back inside. Take time for each step and trust that your body will guide you.*

Clearing a space
Before we put all of this together, there is an optional step to consider. Sometimes, in asking what wants your attention, you find that there are many situations in your life that all demand attention. Another way to say this is that there may be a lot that stands between you

and feeling fine inside. You can put this "a lot" outside your body, by placing each obstacle one by one in an imaginary safe place. This is called "clearing a space." It frees up room inside and enables you to concentrate better. It also gives you more energy and deepens your connection to who you really are. There is one caveat, however. You must promise yourself that you will deal with these problems later on.

There are a number of questions you can use to prompt "clearing a space":

Is there anything in me that is demanding attention at this moment?
Is there anything in my life that is making me feel less than fine?
Is there a place in my body that is keeping me from feeling good?
If I say to myself: "Everything is perfect," do I then feel in my body that this is so? Or is there a place inside that knows otherwise?

Go to each felt sense. Give it some attention. Don't go into it too deeply. But notice it. Stay with it. Find a handle for it. Then take this bodily feeling with its handle and place it outside yourself. Picture yourself putting it in a bucket or box or up on a shelf, whatever feels right to you. Next, repeat the whole process. Ask yourself what else is demanding your attention. Give that some time and interest and then place it outside of you, such as on a cloud, or behind a door. Do this until you start to feel clear. That may happen after one or two cycles. Or it may take five cycles. Trust that a good feeling will come. When it does, take time to enjoy the feeling of clear space inside.

When you start Focusing you may know exactly what situation you want to focus on. In that case, by all means go to that issue and the felt sense in your body that goes with it. However, if you feel full of all different events, problems, and experiences, you may want to clear a space first. Once you've given time and attention to the many things clamoring inside, you can check to see which one needs re-examining. Some questions you can ask at that point are:

Which one feels the heaviest?
Which one hurts most?
What affects me the most?
What bothers me the most?
What is demanding my attention most?

In daily life, clearing a space can be used as an independent micro-process. In this case the goal is not to go deeply into any one feeling, but to free up space for other tasks. Clearing a space is great for reducing stress. You might clear a space before starting work. In cases of physical illness, clearing a space can be an essential healing step.

PUTTING IT TOGETHER: SHORT VERSION

Below you will find a number of sentences which summarize the process of guiding yourself through Focusing. Remember that the order of the steps is not fixed and sometimes steps will overlap. The inner process, or your inner needs, determines the way you will go.

Deepening Your Attention
I am letting my attention go inside.

Clearing a Space if necessary
What is in my way? I am letting it go ... What else is in my way?

Discovering a Felt Sense
What is asking for my attention at this moment? Where do I feel that in my body? How does it feel there?

Finding a Handle
I stay with it with my receptive attention ... I am taking the time to allow a word, memory, wish, smell, or color to come up.

Resonating
I check whether the handle matches my felt sense. Does it all fit? Can my felt sense develop further?

Asking Questions
I check which question fits best here.
What is it all about?
What is the worst of it?
What does it need?
What else in my life is like this?
I explore possibilities until I feel the felt sense "speak" to me.

Receiving
I receive that which is new, no matter how small it seems.
I am attentive to the shift I experience.
I ask myself: Is there anything that is not yet clear, anything that I want to return to later? If so I will give it an imaginary place where I can hold it.
When I am ready, I open my eyes.

FOCUSING WITH A COMPANION

It is possible to focus independently as we have described and have no problems doing so. However, most people find it easier to have someone else present, accompanying them, and giving them the various prompts. It helps concentration and deepens the process.

Your companion's most important task is to be present, listening attentively. You as Focuser say out loud what is going on inside you, without necessarily sharing any details of your problem situation. Your companion reflects back the essence of what you have said, speaking slowly and with an appreciation for the felt sense behind your words. A skilled Focusing companion can suggest which Focusing steps to take and which questions to ask yourself. It is important to emphasize, however, that the Focuser retains full control of the process. It is always up to the Focuser to sense inside whether the companion's suggestion fits. If it doesn't, the Focuser should feel free to dismiss the suggestion openly.

Focusing with a companion can take place within a professional relationship, such as with a professional Focusing trainer (see the *Foreword*). It can also happen in partnership with a friend or acquaintance. In that case no money is exchanged and the partners alternate between the roles of listener and Focuser, so that both have an equal chance to focus.

The sentences and questions below can be used by your Focusing companion. Again, the Focuser is free to say if the question or suggestion doesn't fit, and the companion should try to follow the Focuser's lead.

Put your Attention inside Yourself
Deepening the Attention
Is there an event, situation or question that you want to be with right now?
Let your attention go inside ...

Clearing a Space if necessary
What is in the way of your feeling just fine? ... Let each one of these things go one by one, until you get a bodily-felt sense about something. (Or) Check what is asking for your attention at this moment ... check where in your body you are reacting to it ... notice how it feels there *in your body.*

Discovering a Felt Sense
What is asking for your attention at this moment? Where in your body are you reacting to that situation? Notice how it feels right there.

Finding a Handle
Stay with it with your attention ... stay connected to that bodily-felt

sense ... take the time to allow a word, sentence, memory, or wish to come up in connection with the felt sense.

Resonating
If something comes, welcome it, check whether it fits; then go back and forth between the felt sense and the handle. Keep doing this until you sense that it fits.

Asking/Exploring
Stay with the felt sense, giving it all your attention.
You may want to ask it a question. Check inside to see if one of these fits:

What is so .... (add the handle here) about this?
What is this all about?
What is the worst part of this?
Does this remind me of anything else in my life?
Does the felt sense need anything?
If so, what does it need?

Receiving
Receive that which is new.
Affirm that a shift has taken place.
Check whether it is OK to find a stopping place. Is there anything that is not yet clear, anything you might want to come back to? If so, put that some place where you can find it again.
Take the time, if you want, to thank your body for all that has come. When you're ready, let your eyes open.

Complete example

> *Christa and Evert are focusing partners. Christa accompanies Evert, who has chosen to focus on "being a good father."*
> *Evert:* Today I want to focus on wanting to do a good job as a father.
> *Christa:* Wanting to do a good job as a father ... Is there a place in your body that reacts to that?
> *Evert:* There is something deep in my belly ... like a balloon getting bigger.
> *Christa:* There is something deep in your belly ... like a balloon getting bigger.
> *Evert:* All sorts of things are coming up. (*He moves his hand towards his chest.*)
> *Christa:* All sorts of things are coming up in your chest area ... Can you stay right there with your attention?

Evert: Yes ... I notice it here ... *(He puts his hand on his chest)* But this business of doing it well... it's not situated here. Here it feels like something completely different.

Christa: You notice something completely different in your chest. Maybe you can let this feeling know that it's okay that it's here.

Evert: Yes ... it's okay that it's here ... but it stops... the image of the balloon is deflating and moving upward. And here ... *(He puts his hand to his chest)* It stops here.

Christa: Right there at your chest it stops the balloon that is deflating. It might be good to separate these two, to acknowledge both and give them both attention.

Evert: Acknowledging them gives me a tingle right here. *(He points to his throat)*

Christa: Acknowledging both gives you a tingle right there where you're pointing.

Evert: It's like the feeling of a scream saying, "I want — I have to do well as a father." Now it's really coming through, all the way up to my head. My head immediately says: "No, you don't have to."

Christa: Something is coming through like a scream that you want to do well as a father ... from your belly up to your head. Is it okay to listen again to that scream that is coming from the depths?

Evert: It's located very deeply ... under my backside.

Christa: That scream is coming from a very deep place, from under your backside.

Evert: I am noticing this part really clearly now ... my buttocks are pushing against the chair ... it is OK that it flows from very deeply to ... *(He points to his head)*

Christa: It's OK for it to flow from very deeply, from your backside up to your head.

Evert: I guess so, up to the tip of my nose ... Now I am becoming aware of your presence ... from inside I allow it to come.

Christa: Your inside says that you can let it come all the way up to the tip of your nose.

Evert: And that bloated feeling is decreasing ... it's going away ... it's OK to leave ... I am allowed to feel it and to let it come up to here. *(He points to his nose)*

Christa: The bloated feeling is decreasing ... it is flowing ... it is letting itself be felt ... it comes up to the tip of your nose.

Evert: I still want to stay with this flow for a while ... it's not a straight line ... it's more ... *(He makes a winding gesture)*

... sometimes it even comes to here ... *(He points to his armpits)*

Christa:The flow isn't straight. It's like a winding road that even reaches right under your arms ... the flow has all that in it.

Evert:	There is also fear there ... fear of that long road.

Christa:There is fear of that long road ... can you let it know that it is OK that it is there?

Evert:	Yes, it is okay for that fear to be there ... it is fading away.

Christa:By letting the fear know that it is OK to be there, you allow it to fade away ... and it's a long road.

Evert:	Really right up here under my arms ... I notice in my head that it's saying that I must do something ... do something.

Christa:It is flowing in your body and your head tells you to do something... can you check inside whether it is OK to end here?

Evert:	For me there's a big difference between the balloon that is always stuck and the feeling right now.

Christa:You notice a big difference between the feeling of the balloon and the flow that is there now ... that long winding road.

Evert:	I notice that it's very important for me to come back to this at a later point. I am taking this new feeling with me.

Reflection:

• *Do you notice all the different steps in Evert's process?*

• *Can you find the moment when he makes contact with the felt sense?*

• *At what points do you observe him resonating?*

• *Do you see how his body guides the process?*

Appendix

PROTOCOLS

Brief sentences you can use for the Focusing steps
> You bring your attention inside.
> You check what is asking for your attention at this moment.
> Where do you feel that in your body and how does that feel?
> You let a word or image come up with it.
> You stay with it with your attention.
> You give it the opportunity to express itself with a word, sentence, image, memory, wish, smell, or color.
> You check whether it fits exactly: the felt sense and the handle which has come, so that the felt sense can develop further.
> You are attentive to the bodily-felt shift.
> You receive that which is new, no matter how small it is.
> You anchor this felt shift, so that you can find it again.
> If there is something that is not clear yet and that you want to get back to, then give it an imaginary place.
> Open your eyes when you're ready to do so.

Listening in the mirroring mode
> Mirror the bodily-felt sense.
> Mirror the essence of what has been said.
> Mirror the behavior.
> Mirror in a summarizing way.
> Mirror the emotional quality.
> Mirror a visible change.
> Mirror something that has been discovered.
> Mirror when something new comes.
> Carefully mirror what you assume is going on inside the child at this moment ...

Focusing with the individual child

Creating conditions
> It seems as if something is not going well ...
> Right now I don't have the time to be with you if you should want to be with it inside ... You could ask inside if you want to deal with it at length this evening ... and if it would be alright if I were present ...
> If you want me to be with you, then I am available this evening after eight o'clock ... Just let me know.

In the meantime you can maybe put it outside yourself by drawing it ...

Then it is not in your way when you are going to do your homework ...

Just see what feels good to you.

Listening to the problem or the question

Can you tell me in two sentences what it is about? You know that it is not really necessary ... it is really yours ...

Having the attention go inside

Become aware that your feet are on the ground ... if you wiggle your toes you can feel them better ...

Can you feel that your body is sitting in the chair and that your body is touching the back of the chair and the seat?

Can you feel your hands? Otherwise you move them a little ... Can you feel your breathing going in and out ... Now let your attention sink inside ... if you want, you can close your eyes ...

When you are ready to go on, you may indicate that with a movement of your hand.

How does it feel inside about the problem or the question?

Imagine again what happened today ...

Notice where you feel that in your body now that you are recalling it ...

Take time to check how it feels there in your body ...

Staying with it from the bodily-felt sense

Can you be friendly with it? Can you stay with it with your full attention?

Hearing the inner story or symbolizing it with a word, an image, a color

Check whether this [word or image or color] is exactly right ...

Check between the feeling inside and that word or image ... Maybe it still has something else to say ...

Noticing the shift, keeping in contact with it, receiving and anchoring it

Do you notice that sigh? ... How does it feel inside now?

Can you stay with it with your friendly attention and really receive it?

Teaching Focusing to a group

Discovering sensory awareness in your body

Stamp with your feet ... then feel with your hand how your heart

is beating ...
Pull your shoulders up as high as you can ... up to your cheeks ...
How does that feel? How deeply do you feel that in your body?
Now let your shoulders drop ... Do you notice the difference?
Clench your fists ... feel what is happening in your body.
Clench your teeth ... What do you feel? How does that feel? How
far does that go into your body?
What happens in your body when you imagine that you go very
high on the swing?

Gently stroke the upper side of your arm with the tips of your
fingers ... and the underside ... Do you notice the difference?
Now scratch with your nails ... without hurting yourself ... go over
the upper side of your arm ... and over the underside ... do you
notice a difference inside your body ... your belly or your chest?
Listen to your breathing and feel with your hand on your belly how
it goes up and down.

What happens inside when you imagine that you bite into a slice of
lemon ... and now into something sweet ... do you notice the
difference in your body?
Listen attentively to everything you hear ... open your ears ... Feel
what happens inside with you now.
Look at this image with a little stare ... keep looking ... nice plant
... flowers ... Notice that there is more and more that you are
noticing ... What is happening inside now?

Letting the attention go inside

Can you feel that both your feet are on the floor?
Sometimes it helps when you wiggle your toes, so that you can
feel them better ...
Feel that your body is sitting in the chair ... can you feel that your
back is touching the back of the seat?
Can you feel where your hands are? Otherwise you move them a
little ...
Feel your shoulders ...
Feel how your breath goes in and out ...
If you want you can close your eyes ...
Now let your attention sink inside ...

Tracking a problem

What happens to you when something nasty has happened and
that nasty thing is in the way of your feeling good? Is your first
reaction just like mine? We don't want that nasty feeling in our

body at all ...

We try to push it away ... to forget it by doing other things ... maybe naughty things ... You think that all other children are stupid or rotten ... Then an angry feeling is added inside us ... We feel short-changed ... disappointed ... resentful.

The result of such a feeling is that everything gets stuck inside ... It becomes harder and harder in our hearts ... how do we get out of this?

Shall we do something different about it today? Has anyone come across such a spot inside? Where the angry place is located ... where it is stuck? Who has already experienced something like that?

We let our attention sink back inside again just as we learned last time. It becomes easier and easier to do that.

Being friendly to what comes

Now say to yourself inside: "Hello, nice child ..." "Hello ..." and then you softly mention your name.

Feel what happens inside ... Does anything change?

Inside yourself you search for something that is angry or sad. You search for where there is something that is in the way of feeling fine ...

Then we say something nice to it. Like: "Know that you are inside there grumbling ... that you are angry or sad or ... I am coming to sit with you and will wrap my arms around you ..."

Do you notice anything changing in your inside feelings now?

Take time to draw that changed feeling ... give it a color ... Your hand knows how it wants to go ...

Creating a safe place/color

Imagine that you have your favorite soft toy, doll or toy in your arms. How does that feel? Then if something difficult comes ... that needs your attention ... you make an extra connection between you and your soft toy feeling ...

What is a safe color for you? ... a color that helps you ... a color that makes you feel protected. Keep that color in mind when there is something difficult in your life. You can color this color lightly on your paper before you draw the difficult thing ... Let the total color, the total feeling of that color, come into your body ... Now how does it feel on the inside?

Imagine that a safe imaginary place exists ... a place that you can see before your eyes now ... you know that it is good there ... like the inside of you wants this ... It does not have to be a real place ... that place can stay only in your imagination ... Sometimes it helps to draw that safe place so that you can recall it more easily ...

Can you feel the safe feeling of that place in your body?

Discovering the bodily-felt sense of something by imagining and staying with it

Walk as if you were a giant ... Where do you feel that inside? How does that feel?

Walk like a gnome ... Where do you notice that inside? What is different about it?

Stand like a tree ... How do you notice that inside? Where is that feeling located?

How would you feel inside if you had your absolutely favorite soft toy, doll or toy with you now? Where is that feeling?

Imagine something hard ... Check what you feel inside ... Then imagine something soft ...

Imagine someone who is very sweet ...

What do you notice inside when you succeed at something that seemed too difficult at first?

Calling up and drawing the felt sense about something in your imagination

(By giving attention to good feelings and drawing these feelings, they are reinforced and stick around longer.)

You don't have to make a nice drawing. You don't need an eraser ... inside you know what it means.

You can also use the other side of the paper or take a new sheet of paper.

If you have closed your eyes, you can open them to draw.

Imagine that you are on the beach/in the woods/at a nice place ... Pick a location.

What comes up in your body now ... for instance in your belly or your chest?

When you notice a feeling ... you take time to stay with it ... Perhaps a word or an image comes too ... what belongs to it?

Write or draw what you feel inside ... and what has just come ...

You know that it does not have to be a nice drawing ...

Sometimes a color or various colors come that fit the feeling ...

Linking and drawing the pleasant experiences of daily life from the felt sense

Have you experienced something nice or something great recently?

Think about it again now ... Imagine that you are experiencing it again and how nice it was ... it gets calm inside ... You can feel that nice feeling in your body ... Where do you notice it? ...

It may be easier to do with your eyes shut ... let it become very calm ...

(Here you give a quiet sensory exercise and/or the sentences to invite the attention to go inside.)

We can now listen inside and say to that feeling: "Hello, it is nice that you are there."

If some sensation comes into your body, you wait to feel inside what it is like ... What word or color or image goes with it? No matter what comes up inside you, it is OK ... You keep on feeling what there is. Then you can write or draw or color it on your paper ... In that way you can look at it ... Then this nice feeling can stay and even increase.

Linking and drawing the difficult experiences of daily life from the felt sense

(Begin with a few sensory exercises, a preliminary talk and some explanation.)

Everyone has difficult, hard, unpleasant things inside sometimes, something that bothers you ... something that does not feel good in your life ... You can feel that somewhere in your body ... You can notice what is happening inside you ... Being friendly to what is there helps you solve your problems.

I do that too and that helps me to feel better.

Giving attention and drawing unpleasant feelings helps to make these feelings smaller and to let them change ... If you feel a heavy or painful or pinching feeling in your body ... then sometimes it feels as if it will never be nice again in your life ... it seems difficult to listen to other people ... it is difficult to concentrate on your work ...

Sometimes you try very hard not to feel it ... you want to make sure that it does not come out ... you push it down in your body ... for instance by swallowing your tears, which results in a constricted throat ... or by tensing your stomach.

You get a heavy or dull feeling inside ... you have to explode every now and then ... and that bothers you too ... sometimes you don't understand yourself anymore ... and no there is one who understands it ... Do you recognize that sequence?

Now we are going to give attention inside to that heavy, difficult feeling ... If you listen to it in a friendly way you will find that it slowly becomes different ... as you draw all that ...

Sometimes you know which problem or situation is connected to the heavy or dull feeling ... Other times you just have that feeling and you don't know what it is about ...

You wait patiently ... you listen inside your body ... until something comes that tells you what it is about ... because that feeling in your body has a story to tell ... your body gradually discovers:

"yes, that's what it is ..."

These feelings and stories come up very gently if you are calm and friendly to them ... if you stay friendly to everything that comes ... You can say "hello" to them nicely as if you were talking to yourself or to a friend ...

You can draw this problem or this difficult situation ... You know that it doesn't have to be a nice drawing ... you can make it exactly like your hand wants you to make it.

Sometimes that feeling only brings colored stripes, circles or scratches ... That's OK ... When you draw unpleasant, heavy feelings you will find that it feels different inside your body ... You get the chance to look at them... You can feel freer, easy and calmer ... you can breathe better ... You discover that it is good to give attention to those hard feelings.

Staying with "it" so that it can unfold

Calmly look at your paper every now and then ... What has come? Does it fit your feeling inside exactly? Sometimes there is even more ... Take time for that.

Staying in touch with the shift and strengthening the change

Now can you feel what it is like with the new feeling of space ... maybe new power ... new daring ... or something else still ... What is the feeling that has come inside you? Where is it in your body? What does it feel like? Does it have a color or an image? How does it want to be expressed on your paper? Go and draw this new feeling now to reinforce it and hold onto it ...

Clearing a space

(First we help the children to bring their attention inside. Then ask the child to say to herself: "Hello nice child.")

Maybe you have a problem or something difficult ... something that you have experienced today ... yesterday ... or even a long time ago ... maybe something that is coming tomorrow ... something that bothers you right now ...

Notice where you feel that, somewhere in your body ... you have a sad feeling ... an angry feeling ... a scared feeling ... somewhere in your body it feels compressed ... dull ... stabbing ...

Notice how it is with you ... inside your body.

Where do you feel that?

How does that feel inside you? Can you describe that feeling? Does a color or image belong to it? You take the time to draw it ... You can open your eyes ... When you've drawn that difficult thing, then it is on your sheet of paper ... and it is no longer inside you ... You go back to that spot inside your body, where it was ... Does it feel better there? Or does something more need to come?

Often there is more than one thing that is bothering you ... Take the time to feel inside once again ... You can close your eyes if you want ... Let something else come up that is in the way of your feeling fine ... Sometimes it is an unpleasant, hard feeling without your knowing what it is about...

Wait and see if a color belongs to it ... Does that feeling have a color or shape?

You let your hand move over the paper with the pencil or crayon as you stay with that feeling ... so that it comes out onto the paper ... until you feel more room inside ... Then you go back inside a few more times to see what is still there ... what wants to come out ... Each time you notice how it feels more spacious inside ...

Now you can feel a whole open area inside ... You can also draw that ... Maybe you want to do that on a fresh sheet of paper... Maybe it also has a word or an image or colors ... Let the fresh feeling become even stronger ... so that you can hold onto the good feeling even longer.

BIBLIOGRAPHY

Faber, A.F. & Mazlish, E. (1980) *How to Talk so Kids Will Listen & Listen so Kids Will Talk*. New York: Avon Books.

Cornell, A. W. (1996) *The Power of Focusing*. California: New Harbinger Publications.

Gendlin, E.T. (1978) *Focusing* (2nd ed, 1981). New York: Bantam Books.

Goleman, D. (1995) *Emotional Intelligence: Why it can matter more than IQ.* New York: Bantam Books.

Gordon. T. (1970) *Teacher Effectiveness Training: The program proven to help teachers bring out the best in students of all ages.* New York: Three Rivers Press, Random House.

Stapert, M. (1997) *Children Focusing: Guiding and Teaching Children to Focus.* www.focusing.org: children's corner/articles.

Stern, D.N. (1985) *The Interpersonal World of the Infant: A view from psychoanalysis and developmental psychology.* New York: Basic Books.

Stern, D.N (1992) *Diary Of A Baby: What your child sees, feels, and experiences.* New York: Basic Books.

Verliefde, E. (1999) *Groeipijnen in sociaal contact* (Growing Pains in Social Contact). Leuven/Amersfoort: Acco.

The Focusing-Oriented Counselling Primer
Campbell Purton 2007
ISBN 978 1 898059 82 0 £11.00

This new series presents unparalleled, comprehensive descriptions of key counselling approaches in the twenty-first century. Ideal for students requiring a theory bridge between different courses or focused input for comparative essays and integrative theory assignments. *The Focusing-Oriented Counselling Primer* sets new standards as a succinct guide to focusing and focusing-oriented theory and practice for everyone wanting an authoritative synopsis.

Integrating Spirituality in Counselling:
A manual for using the experiential Focusing method
Elfie Hinterkopf 2008
ISBN 978 1 906254 07 0 £13.00

This book describes a model to help clients work through religious and spiritual problems, deepen existing spiritual experiences and bring about new, life-giving connections to spirituality. Through Focusing, the client learns to examine subtle but concrete bodily feelings that are a vital part of spiritual discovery and growth.

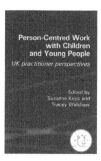

Person-Centred Work with Children and Young People: *UK practitioner perspectives*
Suzanne Keys and Tracey Walshaw (eds) 2008
ISBN 978 1 906254 01 8 £19.00

Love, respect and time for listening to children and young people are what the person-centred psychotherapists and psychologists contributing to this volume have in common. They do this in various settings — primary and secondary schools, a pupil referral unit, voluntary agencies, adoption services, hospitals, a hospice, in the community, and on the streets.

Making and Breaking Children's Lives
Craig Newnes and Nick Radcliffe (eds) 2005
ISBN 978 1 898059 70 7 £14.00

This book examines how children are hurt in modern society. We hear about the effects of early abandonment, abuse and lack of attachment, but find that children's experiences are sanitised through medical diagnoses and frequently the 'help' offered is prescription drugs. A plurality of voices returns to one consistent theme — the importance of psychosocial context — more relevant than ever in the rush to label and prescribe.